POPE FRANCIS

A LIVING LEGACY

JAMES CAMPBELL

DynamicCatholic.com
Be Bold. Be Catholic.®

POPE FRANCIS: A LIVING LEGACY

Copyright © 2014 James Campbell
Published by BEACON PUBLISHING

ISBN: 978-1-937509-78-1

Printed in the United States of America. [2]

Design by Shawna Powell

For more information on this title and other books
and CDs available through The Dynamic Catholic Book Program,
please visit: www.DynamicCatholic.com

The Dynamic Catholic Institute
5081 Olympic Blvd. • Erlanger • KY • 41018
phone: 859–980–7900
email: info@DynamicCatholic.com

TABLE OF CONTENTS

INTRODUCTION

As soon as the name of the new pope was announced on March 23, 2013, the commentators on radio and TV were excited. For the first time in history a Jesuit had been elected pope. Even more exciting, he was the first pope to choose the name Francis. Immediately the commentators assumed that the pope had chosen the name in honor of Saint Francis of Assisi, which Pope Francis confirmed in his press conference the next day.

Saint Francis of Assisi (1181–1226) is perhaps the most well-known and respected saint in Western Christianity. He is seen as a man who epitomized what it means to live like Jesus in his own time and culture. Francis of Assisi was passionate about preaching the Gospel and deeply committed to caring for the poor and needy. He was a man of peace who placed his life on the line to bring the message of Jesus Christ to the Muslim world. With the choice of his name, Pope Francis was telling the world what the principal concerns of his papacy would be.

As a Jesuit, Pope Francis is the spiritual son of Saint Ignatius Loyola (1491–1556), a Spanish soldier who was wounded in battle and discovered his Christian vocation during his convalescence. He went on to take notes on the process of his personal journey, which became the foundation for *The Spiritual Exercises*. A charismatic leader, Ignatius gathered companions and formed with them the Society of Jesus, or Jesuit community. As a Jesuit, Pope Francis was informed by and in his own right became a well-respected director of the exercises for others.

This book explores the legacy of Saint Francis of Assisi and Saint Ignatius Loyola in the life and ministry of Pope Francis. We will see that God raised them up as saints to address the needs of their time. We will also see how Pope Francis is inspired in his papal ministry by their example.

When we look at the worlds of Saint Francis and Saint Ignatius, we discover that they are not all that far from our own time in terms of the hot-button issues facing Christian life. They lived in a time of social change, with ambitious merchants wanting to turn the cold hard cash they earned into political power. They lived in a time when the Mediterranean world was filled with hot spots that flared up all too often into full-scale war. They lived in a time in Western Europe when more men and women were becoming literate and challenging the older way of teaching by word of mouth. In this literate world of education, new ideas and insights led people to critique the way things were done based on a new reading of the Scriptures. Many practices of the Church were criticized for emphasizing the accumulation of riches over the Gospel's focus on poverty. This move into a more literate world had begun in the time of Saint Francis, but was accelerated exponentially with the invention of movable-type print by Johannes Gutenberg in 1450. Within fifty years of Gutenberg's invention, vast libraries of printed books were available for readers to ponder over in the comfort of their homes; they no longer needed to study hand-copied scrolls in a secluded monastery library.

Today we are seeing even more accelerated ways of communication, which make world events instantly accessible, and which have opened up vast libraries of information for everyone to see and judge. This is the communications environment in which Pope Francis is carrying out his papal ministry. We will assess his impact on the world as we continue.

Saint Francis and Saint Ignatius had similar experiences in their respective journeys to Jesus. Each came from a privileged family and wanted to achieve knightly glory. Unlike Francis, who could only aspire to such glory, Ignatius was a full-fledged courtier and soldier, insanely brave against impossible odds. Both saw their hopes shattered in battle. Francis was taken prisoner and held in the most foul of prisons. Ignatius was a prisoner in his own shattered body. In each case the discovery of their own helplessness led to a profound conversion to Jesus Christ, on whom they would depend for the rest of their lives. In his own life Pope Francis experienced a life-threatening illness, which led to the removal of a portion of his right lung. In this period of pain he learned what it meant to offer his suffering to Jesus.

Both Francis of Assisi and Ignatius especially discovered the presence of Jesus Christ in the poor and the sick. They were both men of immense personal charisma, who attracted others to follow the path they had begun toward Jesus. In his environment, Saint Francis was a dynamic preacher, moving the people with his words, actions, and enthusiasm. Ignatius was a great director of souls, through his development and practice of *The Spiritual Exercises.* Following Saint Francis' example, the early friars went into the towns to proclaim the Word of the Lord, helped prepare for the celebration of the Mass, and brought peace to feuding families and neighborhoods. The early Jesuits all had received master's degrees in theology and were called to the world of education and were pioneers in the education of the laity.

Pope Francis has made it clear that he is living the legacy of these great saints. His choice of the name Francis is directly related to his vocation to speak for the poor, the sinners, the immigrants, and the sick, bringing to all of them the continuing message of God's mercy and forgiveness. And he specifically identifies himself as a son of Saint Ignatius, formed by *The Spiritual Exercises*, with Ignatius' fundamental questions on his mind: What have I done for Christ? What am I doing for Christ? What must I do for Christ?

All of us are called to serve God in a particular time and place. We face social, political, family, and religious issues that both limit us in our choices and liberate us to discover where God is calling us to use our talents and abilities most effectively. In this book we will explore how Saint Francis and Saint Ignatius made those choices. We will also see how they inspire Pope Francis in his daily life of prayer and ministry to be all he can be for God and others.

QUESTIONS

What are some of the hot-button issues Catholics are facing today?

What are some of the limitations we experience as Catholics addressing these issues?

What talents and abilities can we offer to God on the path that he is calling us to follow?

How would we answer these questions: What have I done for Christ? What am I doing for Christ? What must I do for Christ?

CHAPTER 1

THE WORLD OF SAINT FRANCIS OF ASSISI

A CLIMATE OF WAR

Saint Francis of Assisi (1181–1226) was born into a culture of continual war. When Francis was six years old, Christian armies were defeated in the Holy Land by the Muslim armies of Saladin; the city of Jerusalem was lost. When he was eight, kings of France, England, and the Holy Roman Empire brought armies to the Holy Land, only to fail to recapture Jerusalem. By the time Francis was twenty-one, in 1202, Pope Innocent III had launched the Fourth Crusade, which never reached the Holy Land. The crusading armies were taken by a fleet from Venice to attack and ultimately sack Constantinople, the center of Eastern Christianity. The crusading knights set up a Western dynasty in Constantinople, which was eventually defeated and thrown out in 1261. As much as any event in the history of Christianity, this has been a lingering source of resentment and disunion between Western and Eastern Christianity.

During this period Pope Innocent III also initiated the Albigensian or Cathar Crusade against cities in southern France. From 1209 to 1229, Cathar cities were put under siege and eventually sacked. This was an extremely ferocious campaign; the Albigensian crusaders showed no mercy to the conquered as they massacred the defeated people in the name of God.

Closer to where Francis was raised, in Assisi, Italy, social, economic, and political differences led to constant skirmishing among the small armies of competing cities and the local aristocracy. The growth of the cities saw the financial and social advancement of the merchant class, men like Francis' father, Peter Bernardone, ambitious to control their own affairs and expand their influence. As the cities worked to expand their authority over the neighboring countryside, they came into conflict with the feudal aristocracy, who wanted to hold on to their land. The growing cities of Italy were also constantly at war with one another. In 1201, when Francis was twenty, he got involved in one of the perpetual skirmishes between the cities of Assisi and Perugia. He proudly marched out clad in knightly armor on a new horse, only to be captured when the superior army of Perugia defeated the army from Assisi.

What we see, then, is a society that had chosen to forget the meaning of peace as they devoted their energies to the habit of war.[1]

SOCIAL BACKGROUND

Since Italy was the principal shipping point for the French and English armies headed for the Holy Land, port cities like Venice were perfectly poised to take advantage: They earned obscene profits from the goods and transport services sold to the crusaders, and then they used the crusaders to help them destroy their Byzantine competition in the eastern Mediterranean. Thus the Italian cities gained even greater control over the trade routes, adding to their riches.

The financial gains of the merchant class led to social ambition. With their success in trading raw materials for finished goods, the merchants had more ready cash to spend and to loan out at high rates. The feudal economy that the merchants sought to replace was primarily a local economy based on the land and artisans to provide for the needs of the aristocracy. The growth of a cash economy caused social tensions as the merchants wanted to see their money grow. This was the first time in human history that the accumulation of money was seen as a value all its own. Up to this time, money was tied to the land and dependent on good weather conditions to support the yearly agricultural harvest. The aristocracy and the Church were usually short of ready cash. With the growth of wealth came political ambition. While they fought the aristocrats, the wealthy merchant commoners wanted to move up in their status and become members of the aristocracy themselves.

Italian cities like Assisi and Perugia became limited urban republics. The newly rich created their own institutions of politics and law. They saw themselves as free men not tied to feudal obligations. Often the local aristocrats were attacked, their castles burned to the ground. With all their goods confiscated, the knights and their families went into exile.

The republics that took control of the cities were limited in the sense that only those with money had any power or influence; the poor were systematically kept in their place. As moneyed people grew their wealth through trade, they also became owners of agricultural lands and were even more rapacious than the former aristocracy in squeezing what profit they could from the farmers. In the cities the poor who worked in menial labor had no protection against the exploitative merchants. [2]

When families entered a city to become artisans or to advance in the trades, they came under the civil jurisdiction of the commune. In this time individual liberty was not understood as the ability to promote one's personal rights against the civil authority. The individual had simply shifted his loyalty from an aristocrat to the commune. The only people whom the aristocracy or the commune did not have control over were the clerics, who were under the authority of the Church.

As the merchant class and its allies of master artisans and lawyers pushed for more political authority, it also became alienated from the Church, whose mind-set was still in the rural environment. The clergy had no answers to new questions members of the moneyed class were asking. The Church condemned usury, the lending of money for interest, which was a good source of income for those who had surplus cash to lend. The Church's view of the world of the cities was also negative, promoting the idea that the truly spiritual person is one who leaves the world for a life of contemplation in a monastic community. These monastic communities fulfilled their vocations by praying for the world, but that did not address a growing spiritual vacuum in the lives of an articulate, rising merchant class. [3]

THE CHURCH

Historians present the years of Francis of Assisi's life as the high point of the Church's secular power. As we have seen, Pope Innocent III called crusader armies into existence and sent them into battle, albeit disastrously in the case of the Fourth Crusade. The pope did not hesitate to use his power to punish kings who disagreed with him. King John of England (1166–1216) was excommunicated from 1209 to 1213 because of a dispute with the pope.

Although Innocent III was worldly and powerful, he also saw the need for reform. In this time, bishops, abbots, and religious communities were large landowners, controlling the wealth of their holdings. For a poor but ambitious and learned man, the Church was an admirable career choice, as there was a greater chance for advancement on merit. The money collected by the Church was usually used to pay the benefices or stipends of the mostly aristocratic clergy. Upper clergy could be immensely wealthy, using benefices to support their lifestyle. Bishop Guido of Assisi owned half the city and was quite vigorous in the courts to protect his holdings.

Noble families usually saw Church institutions such as monasteries as a great opportunity to place their second sons, giving them an income and a chance for advancement. There was a great deal of prejudice against incipient religious communities not tied to the land. We see the hostility toward these communities in the story of young Thomas Aquinas (1225–1274). Saint Thomas Aquinas was from an important aristocratic family, who wanted to place him at Monte Cassino, the most venerated Benedictine monastery, with the goal of him eventually becoming the abbot. Thomas infuriated them by becoming a Dominican friar, at that time a new order without proper pedigree, in the opinion of his family. His family imprisoned him for a time, and only later relented to let him live as a Dominican.

The structure of the Church was based on the ideals of monastic life—a turning away from the world, which was seen as evil. The bishops and upper clergy's views on their place in the world were (to use Pope Francis's term) self-referential, as they were more concerned with protecting their goods than with proclaiming the Word to the world. The Mass, including the Scripture readings, was celebrated in Latin. The spiritual life of the people in the cities was limited to the homilies and the sacred images in the stained-glass windows. As the new, literate, and highly articulate merchant class grew, the Church had little to offer; there was a spiritual vacuum, as few spiritual practices existed for their daily lives. While they participated in the festivals celebrating the patrons of their cities, the Church had little to offer them for growing in a personal spiritual life.

Those especially left out of the new society were the poor and the ill, particularly the ones suffering from leprosy and other skin diseases. In the rural environment of feudal life it was the responsibility of the aristocracy, who controlled the land and sources of wealth, to care for the poor. There was also the voluntary poor, the monks who turned their backs on the wealth of the world but supported themselves with their landed estates. [4]

In the emerging environment of the merchant class, any feudal obligations were set aside, and no one took responsibility for the poor and marginalized. It was the genius of Francis of Assisi and his contemporary Saint Dominic Guzman (1170–1221), founder of the Dominicans, to address the need to evangelize and catechize the new age, offering a new awareness of what the life, death, and resurrection of Jesus meant in terms of caring for the poor.

THE FAMILY OF FRANCIS

Francis' father, Peter Bernardone, was one of the new merchants who became wealthy through commerce or manufacturing. Peter specialized in manufacturing colorful brocaded cloaks, vests, furred hats, gold collars, and gray stocking caps, using the raw materials he purchased in Northern Europe. [5] He was primarily a merchant in textiles, but he also had cash deposited or on loan with interest. He invested in real estate within the confines of Assisi. As the city grew and the economy improved, Peter profited from his investments. A great deal of his wealth also came with the dowry of his wife, Pica. With good business sense, Peter was able to make the money grow.

In 1181, when Francis was born, Peter was on a trip to France, buying goods to resupply his inventory. Francis' mother first named him John, but Peter renamed him when he returned from his trip. The baby's baptism most likely took place on Saturday, March 28, 1182. At that time it was the practice in Italian cites to baptize healthy infants on the afternoon of Holy Saturday. Following baptism, Francis would have been anointed by the bishop. The next day, as was the custom of the time, he would have received his first Communion before the altar of the cathedral at the end of the Easter Vigil. This was a festive occasion for the community, with Peter and Pica proudly walking with Francis' godparents, carrying Francis through the town plaza to a great feast celebrating the occasion. [6]

Francis grew up as a young man full of charm, stories, and songs. He was a leader among his friends, who were only too ready to spend his family's wealth on their frivolous pursuits. Peter no doubt was not happy watching his money go out the door, but he tolerated it because he wanted to impress the noble class, whose sons were Francis' followers. It was a matter of pride for Peter to have the money for Francis to spend. [7]

QUESTIONS

What does it mean to have grown up in a society in which there is a "habit of war"?

In Saint Francis' day, the Church was not always in tune with giving the people what was necessary for their spiritual life. What needs in our society do you think the Church has to address today?

How closely do we identify with the ambitions of Peter Bernardone and his willingness to spoil his son?

Where can we find God in the midst of those ambitions?

CHAPTER 2

FRANCIS' JOURNEY

Peter Bernardone brought the teenage Francis on his trips
north to France and the Low Countries (present-day Belgium
and the Netherlands) to purchase the raw materials for his finished goods. Peter was a good and faithful man but also an
ambitious one who wanted to protect the fortune he accumulated..

As a young man on these journeys, Francis was introduced
to his father's business and exposed to the French mercantile
system and culture. Traveling in a well-armed caravan for
their safety, Francis mingled with the crowds of merchants
and minstrels. He learned not only the French language but
also the popular songs, poems, and romantic tales from the
troubadours who gathered to entertain the merchants. He
loved to imitate these songs, and they became the model for
his own poetry. [8]

During his teen years Francis was the most popular young
man in Assisi. He did not hesitate to use his father's fortune
to advance himself on the social scene. As a talented poet and
singer, he entertained his friends and paid for their parties. Yet
while Francis was quite the man-about-town, there is no indication that he was a rake or womanizer; he treated everyone
with courtesy.

Francis aspired to live out the courtly virtues attributed to
knightly chivalry. The class of knights in European history
began as a bunch of thugs on horses, building castles (which

we find romantic) to control the countryside and bring the farmers under their heel as serfs. In order to give the knights a more Christian moral code, at the end of the twelfth century there developed the ideal of knightly chivalry (from *cheval-erie,* meaning "horse soldiery"). The chivalric ideal taught that knights should protect those who could not protect themselves, such as widows, children, and elders. Knights were taught to be loyal and generous, and to respect the honor of women.

Since knightly glory was won on the battlefield, it was probably unreasonable for Francis, the poet and storyteller, to imagine he could fulfill such a role, yet it is this ideal of knightly courtesy that we see influencing him as a young man. One day he was approached by a beggar while he was at work, and Francis brushed him off. Then he felt ashamed for not treating the man with courtesy. He rushed out of the shop, found the man, and gave him what money he had.[9]

FRANCIS GOES TO WAR

Francis had a chance to show his knightly resolve when one of the perpetual feuds between Perugia and Assisi broke out into war. He immediately volunteered to join the forces of Assisi, dressed in the regalia of a knight. Peter Bernardone paid the enormous expense of Francis' armor, weapons, and a horse, and Francis went off to war to make his name. It did not go well; the forces of Assisi were overmatched and slaughtered. Francis survived the battle, but not the humiliation of being taken prisoner. For six months the commune in Perugia did not tell Assisi how many had been killed or captured. They finally announced the names of those alive so they could be ransomed, a process that took another year. As a prisoner, Francis was lucky to survive the experience.

Conditions were appalling by any standard. Prisoners were confined in perpetual darkness in a subterranean vault and subsisted on a meager diet of stale leftovers and tainted water; there was nothing like a latrine or facilities for washing, and the place was brutally cold in winter and cruelly airless in summer. It was an ideal incubator for malaria, tuberculosis and all manner of bacterial and viral diseases; as it happened, many prisoners did not survive the ordeal.[10]

The Francis who returned to Assisi was a more thoughtful young man, aware of the hollowness of his former life. He was bedridden with the diseases he had caught in prison. He eventually returned to work in his father's business, but not with the gaiety and enthusiasm he'd had before the war. He was no longer the young man who sparkled at every party.

When another opportunity for military glory emerged, this time to fight in the name of the pope, Francis purchased another set of knight's armor and a horse and left Assisi with the full intention of making up for his failed experience. However, once he got on the road, he felt the emptiness of his dreams. He shared with a companion that in answering the summons of the pope, he was not following the path of greatest glory.

The upshot of the conversation was that he now realized that following a minor vassal rather than the lord in charge of the expedition was not a formula for glory. Later recounting turned this "lord" into God in heaven, but such a spiritual motivation for heading home seems far from Francis's unsettled state of mind. Whatever happened on the fateful night, Francis abandoned returning to the military life as the solution to his problems. With that option closed, he was now truly adrift.[11]

Francis could go no farther. In knightly generosity he gave away his newly purchased armor and horse to a poor knight. So went the last expensive investment Peter Bernardone made in his son.

FRANCIS AT SAN DAMIANO

On his way back to Assisi, hiding from his family out of embarrassment, Francis stopped and prayed at the run-down local chapel of San Damiano. While praying, he had a vision of the Lord telling him to rebuild the Church. Francis took this to mean the chapel he was in. He immediately went to purchase the stones he needed for the job. He financed them by selling his father's cloth. When he brought the money to the priest at San Damiano, the priest refused to take it, not wanting to face the wrath of Peter Bernardone. Francis responded by throwing the money away.

Peter Bernardone had been patient during Francis' long period of convalescence. But with his son's theft and sale of merchandise, Peter had had enough. Francis' irresponsible actions were threatening the fortune his father was working so hard to preserve for his family. Peter went to Bishop Guido to complain about Francis' behavior. Bishop Guido told Francis that it was unjust to spend his father's money, no matter how sincere he was in wanting to repair the chapel.

Francis decided to return to his father everything that he had been given. He stripped off the clothes he was wearing. He said Peter Bernardone was no longer his father, but henceforth God would be his father. Bishop Guido covered Francis with a cloak, signifying that Francis was now the responsibility of the Church. The bishop gave him a tunic and rope to tie it, and Francis left the building with nothing but his life and faith that God would provide. Peter Bernardone picked up the clothes Francis had left on the ground and went home. This is the last record we have concerning Francis' parents.

FIRST STEPS IN A NEW JOURNEY

Francis left Assisi for San Damiano to fulfill his call to rebuild the chapel. He would live by begging for his food and for money to buy the stones needed to repair the church. His would be a life of prayer and solitude.

Then Francis saw a group of lepers outside town. For his whole life, he had kept his distance from these disfigured human beings. Lepers had to carry a wooden clapper to warn people that they were on the road. But the foul smell of their decaying flesh and open sores probably was sufficient warning of their presence.

When Francis saw this group of lepers, instead of running away, he ran to them. He not only embraced them, but began ministering to them, carrying them to the river to clean the pus out of their open wounds. Instead of disgust, Francis experienced joy and compassion. He was beginning to discover the nature of true nobility and chivalry. Human nobility was not to be found in glorious victories in battle mounted on a horse, nor in keeping company with kings and princes. True nobility is found in service to the weakest, most disfigured and marginalized of society.[12]

Later Francis would write in his testament, "The Lord led me among the lepers and I did mercy to them." In his personal encounter with those who suffer the most, he began to understand the meaning of the crucified Jesus he was meditating upon in the chapel of San Damiano.

> This fateful association with the most despised part of humanity was going to enable Francis to find God in the person of Christ, who had identified himself with the misery of the world by becoming united with the inhuman suffering of these marginalized persons. Francis' reaction is captured in the little phrase in the Testament where he mentions this decisive encounter: "And I did mercy to them."[13]

In serving the most wretched of the earth, Francis was reintroducing them to the human community. In this way he was extending the idea of justice in human and social relationships to include all of God's children.

THE FIRST BROTHERS

As Francis went about his business of repairing the chapel at San Damiano and other local churches, he initially supposed that this was how he would live the rest of his life, in solitude. Then other men began to come and ask to join him. They included a rich man, Bernard of Quintavalle, who was experiencing the meaninglessness of his wealth. He gave it away so he could join Francis. Then came a farmer, a knight, a teacher, a jurist. For a time, these men worked the fields for their living, and worked with Francis to restore the churches. Francis welcomed them, but as yet he did not have a vision of what this little community could become.

TAKE NO GOLD NOR SILVER

In April 1208, a vision for his community was revealed to Francis and two of his companions. They asked the local parish priest at San Nicolò di Piazza to reveal God's will for them by opening the Bible three times and reading them random verses from the Scripture. The church did not have a complete Bible, so the priest used his altar missal (which can now be seen at the Walters Art Museum, in Baltimore).

As was customary, the priest opened the missal three times, read the passage in Latin, and interpreted the text and its meaning. The first reading, from Mark 10:17–21, contained the verse in which Jesus tells his disciples to sell what they have, give to the poor, and follow him. In the second reading, from Luke 9:1–6, Jesus instructs his disciples to take nothing on their journey—no staff, no bag, no bread, and no money—and to wear only a single tunic. In the third reading, from Matthew 16:24–28, Francis and his friends heard the verse "If any want to become my followers, let them deny themselves and take up their cross and follow me."

Francis and his companions memorized these texts. In them they had found the vision of who God was calling them to be as individuals and as a community.[14] He wrote these scriptures into regulations for religious when he founded the Secular Franciscan Order.

MEETING POPE INNOCENT III

Francis wanted to send his brothers to preach this simple message of following Jesus Christ. The Church's experience of laymen preaching the Gospels in this period was not always positive. Sincere laypeople would begin preaching but then their rhetoric would turn into blistering attacks on the clergy and the Church. When Church authorities heard about Francis sending his friars out to preach, they were suspicious.

Francis went to Rome with some of his companions to seek approval from Pope Innocent III for his new order. In 1210, the pope was impressed with the regulations Francis had written and gave approval to the ministry of Francis and his friars.

In their preaching, Francis and the friars never attacked the institutional Church or the clergy. Instead they preached the joy of following Christ in service to the world.

FRANCIS AND ISLAM

In the years following Pope Innocent III's approval of Francis' rule, many more men came to the community to become friars. For Francis himself they were years of travel and serious illness. Not having a talent for administration, he left that task to others. What he wanted to do was go to the Holy Land and achieve martyrdom preaching among the Muslims.

The Fifth Crusade (1213–1221) took the battle to Egypt. In 1219 Francis went there on a mission to bring the Gospel to the Muslims. This was his third attempt to reach out to the Muslim community. The first was in 1211, when his trip to the Holy Land was turned back by a storm. The second was a trip to Morocco in an unsuccessful attempt to speak to the sultan there.

It was Francis' great hope that Muslims could be converted to Christianity not through the sword, but through the example of Christians who lived out the values of Jesus Christ. He discovered to his dismay that the crusaders were more interested in fighting for what they could pillage from the Muslims.

The crusaders even turned down a peace offer that would have included free access to Jerusalem. [15]

During a period of truce between the Christian and Muslim forces, Francis and his companion crossed the lines of battle and requested a meeting with the Muslim ruler Sultan al-Kamil. Francis discovered that the sultan was an educated man. He was impressed by al-Kamil's demeanor and readiness to listen. The sultan was moved by Francis' faith and holiness. He even brought in Muslim scholars to debate with Francis.

Francis spent several days discussing matters of faith with Sultan al-Kamil and Muslim teachers. The sultan allowed him to preach to the Muslim soldiers, which was an unthinkable privilege at the time. At the end of the truce, Francis and his companion left on friendly terms with the Muslims, refusing to take a large sum of money from the sultan.

Sultan al-Kamil wanted to negotiate with the Christian crusaders and arrive at a peace treaty, but the Christians refused. Francis was greatly distressed that the truce ended and bitter fighting continued between Christians and Muslims.

In a final battle between the Christian and Muslim armies, the crusaders were defeated and their armies surrendered. Al-Kamil agreed to an eight-year peace treaty. Franciscans were now allowed to be stationed in the Holy Land; they remain custodians of the Holy Land today.

FINAL YEARS

When Francis returned from his travels to the crusading lands, he found that the Franciscan community had grown to more than three thousand friars. This was beyond his capacity to lead. He resigned his position as head of the community and retired to a hermitage.

THE FIRST CHRISTMAS CRÈCHE

In the winter of 1223 Francis was in the town of Greccio. To prepare for the Christmas celebration, he had a local carpenter erect a grotto near the altar of the church, modeled after the stable in Bethlehem. In the straw-filled grotto Francis placed a live ox and ass, and an image of the child Jesus.

On Christmas Eve the townspeople gathered by torch-light to view the first Christmas crèche, and the friars sang the chants for the Vigils of the Nativity just before Midnight Mass. Serving as deacon for the Mass, Francis sang the Gospel and preached on the birth of Jesus. [17]

In creating the crèche, Francis wanted to emphasize the humanity of Jesus as one of us, as one who was humble enough to become human for the sake of our salvation. The idea of the crèche depicting the Nativity of Jesus quickly spread throughout Europe and remains the iconic image for celebrating the Christmas season.

FINAL DAYS AND HYMN TO NATURE

Since his days of imprisonment, Francis' health was never good. The stringent diet he imposed upon himself and the lack of modern medical care for his ailments meant that at times he was ill for years and unable to move from his bed.

Yet in spite of all of these ailments, Francis traveled on foot to Rome, and then by sea to the Holy Land and to Egypt. In the travel conditions at that time, he was probably exposed to the weather as the galleys or galleons rolled back and forth in the tide and at the whims of the wind and rain. There were no luxury cabins, and he was responsible for bringing his own food. Aboard the precarious wooden ships, fire for cooking was often not available if the weather was too rough.

Francis moved forward, following the vision God had planted in his heart as his health worsened and he grew increasingly blind. His last years were filled with constant physical torment, which he suffered in solitude. During this time, he meditated increasingly on the Passion of the Lord. It is said that Francis was the first to receive the imprint of the wounds of Christ in his flesh, or the stigmata.

For Francis this period of immense physical suffering was also a time of immense joy, because he knew that he had been "saved by the sacrifice of Christ on the cross and by his glorious wounds, which allow the human person to have access to life through the flowing of blood and water."[18]

Finally, near death, Francis dictated the most beautiful of his songs, the "Canticle of the Sun."

Most High Almighty Good Lord,
Yours are praise, glory, honor and all blessing.

To You alone, Most High, do they belong,
And no man is worthy to mention You.

Be praised, my Lord, with all Your creatures,
Especially Sir Brother Sun,
Who is daylight, and by him
You shed light on us. And he is beautiful and radiant with great splendor. Of You, Most High, he is a symbol.

Be praised, my Lord for Sister Moon and the Stars.
In heaven You have formed them clear and bright and
fair.

Be praised, my Lord, for Brother Wind
And for air and cloud and clear and all weather,
By which You give Your creatures nourishment.

Be praised, my Lord, for Sister Water,
For she is very useful, humble, precious and pure.

Be praised, my Lord, for Brother Fire,
By whom You light up the night,
For he is fair and merry and mighty and strong.

Be praised, my Lord, for our Sister Mother Earth,
Who sustains and rules us
And produces varied fruits with many-colored flowers
and plants.

Praise and bless my Lord
And give Him thanks and serve Him with great humility. [19]

Francis died October 3, 1224, at the age of forty-four. He was
canonized in Assisi by Pope Gregory IX in 1228.

QUESTIONS

How were Francis' failures signs of grace in his life?

How do we accept the misfortunes and illness we experience in life?

Where did Francis most vividly discover the presence of Jesus in the world?

What does Saint Francis have to teach us about relating to Muslims?

What does the "Canticle of the Sun" tell us about Saint Francis' spirituality?

CHAPTER 3

FRANCIS OF ASSISI'S LEGACY

It is no surprise that one of Pope Francis' early trips outside Rome was to visit the town of Assisi, to pray in the basilica and other shrines in the town and to show clearly how his papal ministry is inspired by Saint Francis of Assisi and Saint Clare of Assisi. Pope Francis sees Saint Francis not as a figure from the distant past but as someone who left a living legacy, both in the Franciscan religious communities he inspired and in his teachings and example. A close reading of Pope Francis' words and actions shows how they resonate with Saint Francis' teachings and achievement.

FRANCIS AND THE GOSPELS

Francis was raised as a merchant, and had no academic schooling beyond his early teen years. He was not a theologian, his knowledge of Latin was poor, and what he learned of God he learned from hearing the Gospels and, later, praying his Breviary every day. In other words, his access to the divine mysteries was through sources that are available to all who pay attention to the Gospel readings at Mass, and who take the time to read the Divine Office. But everything that Francis heard or read he took to his heart; it was the Word of God calling him forward.

LOVING THE TRIUNE GOD

For Francis, Christian life meant entering more intimately into the life of the triune God: Father, Son, and Holy Spirit. When he stripped himself of the clothes his father had given to him, he declared that God was now his father. His way to the Father was by following and imitating his son, Jesus Christ, inspired by the Holy Spirit. He wrote of the Trinitarian life in his "Letter to the Entire Order":

> Almighty, eternal, just and merciful God,
> Grant us in our misery (the grace)
> To do for You alone
> What we know You want us to do
> And always
> To desire what pleases You.
> Thus,
> Inwardly cleansed,
> Interiorly enlightened,
> And inflamed by the fire of the Holy Spirit,
> May we be able to follow
> In the footprints of Your beloved Son,
> our Lord Jesus Christ.
> And,
> By Your grace alone, may be alone,
> May we make our way to You,
> Most High,
> Who live and rule
> In perfect Trinity and simple Unity,
> and are glorified, God most powerful,
> forever and ever.
>
> Amen. [20]

Francis experienced the Trinity as the God of the Bible, surrounded by angels and archangels. God was all powerful and all merciful; he sent his son among us so that the Son could lead us to the Father. Jesus is the bridge between God and us. Through Jesus God manifested himself to the lowliest. [21]

> For the early Franciscans, a nice, "clean" God, detached from the suffering of creation was not the God that captured their hearts. Rather, they met the God of humble love, bent over in love in the cross of Jesus Christ. It was for this God that they sacrificed everything, assured that suffering would lead them to a greater union of love. According to Patricia Hampl, Francis "was a joyous mystic who needed to suffer the great pain of his age." Francis needed to be with the poor and marginalized, with the lepers and those rejected by society because that is where he believed God truly to be. [22]

THE PATH TO GOD

The path to God for Francis is through the senses, by which the insights we have pass into the body and lead to the soul: "To hear and to see were especially to be desired. It was while he was gazing upon the crucifix of San Damiano and meditating on the sufferings of the Crucified that he heard the words of Christ addressed to him." [23]

For Francis God was not distant, but was an invisible God with his face turned toward the human family. In the blessing Francis gave to Brother Leo, quoting from the book of Numbers (6:24–26), Francis says that God shows his countenance: "May the Lord bless and keep you; may he show his face to you and be merciful to you. May he turn his countenance to you and give you peace! May the Lord bless you, Brother Leo." [24]

Francis describes his experiences of God as a sensation of warmth and light, a light that illuminates the angels and saints and whose warmth we can feel through the warmth of the sun: "[God] is perceptible only through his concrete, palpable manifestations: nature, parchment leaves on which his name is written, churches of stone where the Eucharist is celebrated, the bread and wine that are the tangible signs of his Incarnation and infinite love for the human race." [25]

JESUS CHRIST

For Francis the summit of God's love is seen in the crucified Jesus. Francis made his own the prayer of the liturgical office of the "finding" of the cross as it was celebrated in his time: "We adore you, Lord Jesus, and we bless you because by your holy cross you have redeemed the world." [26]

Francis' devotion to the crucified Christ was not simply admiration and gratitude for what Christ had done for him, for the more he identified with the needs of the poor and the marginalized, the more he could identify the crucified Jesus' presence in the world, in their suffering. Francis reinterpreted the true glory of God in the world, not in the world of courtly or commercial success, but in that of the poor and marginalized.

> Seeing God in the wounds of the Crucified drew Francis to a new level of compassion and to sharing his goods, indeed, his very self, with the other. Bonaventure writes that "to poor beggars he wished to give not only his possessions but his very self, sometimes taking off his clothes . . . ripping them in pieces to give to them." The encounter with Christ as other, therefore,

imparted to Francis a new openness and freedom. Embraced by the compassionate love of God, Francis was liberated within and went out to embrace the other in love. [27]

In the class-driven world of the Middle Ages, a person's dignity was judged by social position. In establishing the Franciscan communities Francis treated all men and women as brothers and sisters. This was how he saw that God wanted all people to live with one another; to break the bonds of these relationships was a sin. Francis called his followers to live in these relationships that might include those who in other circumstances would be excluded. As they gathered in prayer and community, the friars and nuns discovered that the Word of God spoken to them was experienced as the word of life. [28]

JOURNEYING WITH CHRIST

As we have seen, Francis and his companions were called to follow Jesus two by two.

> When winter came, he decided to undertake a new crusade with his sons. Calling them together, he said to them: "Since it is God's will for us to work, not only for our own salvation, but also for the salvation of others, we will go all over the world to preach—by example, even more than in words—penitence and peace. Among those whom you will meet, some will give you a good reception and will listen to you; but the greater part will reject you and revile you. Reply humbly to those who question you; and as for those who shall persecute you, show them your gratitude." [29]

When the brothers traveled, they stopped and prayed at the crosses and churches to which they had a particular devotion. When they entered some churches they found disorder, the sacred vessels lying about unkempt and dirty, pages of the sacred texts strewn about the sanctuary. The friars cleaned up the messes they found so the Mass could be celebrated in an appropriate manner. When the brothers entered a town, they preached peace, telling the townspeople to fear and love the Creator of heaven and earth and observe the commandments. They mostly taught by example, as "Francis had no time for useless or idle words; he recommended to his brothers that they express themselves 'in few words' and to live first by example what they were going to preach." [30]

FINDING GOD IN EVERYDAY LIFE

Unlike the monastic experience of withdrawing from the world to grow closer to God, Francis and his brothers followed the path of seeking God in everyday life. The world was their cloister.

All too often the search for God is in the corridors of power. Francis instead found a God of crucified love, in the lives of the poor and marginalized, in the lives of the people they preached to and loved.

> To know this God we must let go of our fears, expectations and speculations of what God is like and freely enter the mystery of the cross. We can enter this mystery by entering into our own hearts, the mystery of our own humanity with its joys and sorrows, gifts and wounds. Here is where God dwells, in the midst of our fragile humanity, the God who bends low to embrace us in love. [31]

Saint Francis' prayer in the Holy Spirit following the path of Jesus to the Father led him to see God in the concrete reality of everyday life. Anyone suffering became for him a visible expression of God's overflowing love. What was bitter became sweet.

Those moments of transcendence that engage us in the random moments of the ordinary are the privileged experiences of God in our world, or the presence of the living Christ. The experience of seeing Christ in others is the result of openness to the power of God's spirit working in and through all people. It is the reorientation of one's view from the lofty and mighty to the simple and humble, even to the most despised and neglected among us. [32]

CHRISTIAN JOY

Although Francis and his brothers lived a rigorous life, he did not want to see sad faces. He believed that sad faces meant people were troubled by their sins. They were to go to God for forgiveness and return with happy faces.

> Francis said that "spiritual joy is as necessary to the soul as blood is to the body." A gloomy man for him was hardly a citizen of the city of God. Melancholy he dubbed "the Babylonian evil, which plays the devil's game, and renders us vulnerable to his shafts. But for the servant of God who strives to live in joy, the devil's pains go for naught; and he leaves him, finding no entrance to his soul." [34]

Francis' deep sense of joy came out of his conviction of how much he was loved by God. In Jesus' Incarnation and Passion, God has entered into the depths of human experience and brought to all of humanity the saving grace of God. Thanks to Jesus, God took on a human face. How can we not be joyful to have such a savior reaching out to us to bring us home to the Father?

The joy generated by repentance and forgiveness of sins has also become a consistent theme in the homilies of Pope Francis.

> The joy of God is not the death of the sinner, but the life of the sinner. And how far from this were those who murmured against Jesus, how far from the heart of God! They didn't know Him. They thought that being religious, being good people meant always being well-mannered and polite, and often pretending to be polite, right? This is the hypocrisy of the murmuring. But the joy of God the Father, in fact, is love. He loves us. "But I'm a sinner, I've done this and that and the other!" "But I love you anyway, and I go out searching for you, and I bring you home." This is our Father. Let's reflect on this. [35]

PREACHING TO THE PEOPLE

When we looked at the social background of the rising merchant class in the Italian cities, we also noted that the medieval Church in many ways did not speak to their needs. In the great liturgies in the cathedrals and local churches, the readings were done in Latin, with any interpretation dependent on the sermon. All too often the solemn preachers, confident in their own superiority, would sprinkle their sermons with numerous Latin citations that could leave the assembly impressed, but not feeling as if they had been fed.

The homilies that Francis and his brothers gave were not presented in formal discourses. They looked for words that would directly impact the lives of their listeners. Also, following Francis' example, the brothers showed with their actions that they were not "superior" to their listeners, but were partners in faith, walking the path with them: "We can say without exaggeration that by refusing the amalgam that had been created in the medieval Church between the transmission of the word of God and cultural superiority, Francis has virtually created in the West—for the first time since the Dialogues of Gregory the Great—a religious culture of poverty." [36]

In his preaching, Francis was very much a dramatist, acting out the stories that he was communicating. When proclaiming the Gospel, he used gestures and movements to punctuate his words.

> Man of the spoken word, Francis communicated equally with his body, which was constantly in motion. Sometimes he translated the sufferings of the Crucified into mime, sometimes he stripped himself publicly to represent the nakedness of Christ on the cross and shocked his audiences so as to lead them, in their own way, to "follow naked the naked Christ," having wept for themselves and their sins. More than just a sermon, it was a veritable performance during which the body of Francis became the very place where the sacred representation of the Crucified was being played out, a kind of living emblem of Christ. [37]

Francis spoke not only to the head, but to the heart. After his sermons the listeners did not leave with intellectual formulas or memorized quotes; they left with the vivid memory of the story Francis was telling, of Jesus Christ crucified for their salvation. They also now intuitively knew that the way of following Christ would be to act out in their own lives Jesus' compassion for all, especially for the poor.

WHAT SAINT FRANCIS GAVE THE CHURCH

At a time when the Church was still primarily speaking and preaching Latin, there was little attention given to the spirituality of everyday life. Francis (and Dominic) stepped into this vacuum and preached to the people in their own language and vocabulary, showing them the path to holiness in everyday life.

In this way Francis helped the people to recognize the sacredness of their own language, and opened up for them the emotional resonance between their own lives and the lives of the crucified Jesus. He also made possible the development of devotions in the vernacular that would feed the people's spiritual lives. "Through his witness, he freed the dramatic dimension of the Italian language, its absence of restraint in the expression of feelings—from love to indignation—and this fervent enthusiasm for justice and humility which would find their strongest expression at the beginning of the fourteenth century in the Franciscan poet Jacopone da Todi." [38]

FRANCIS THE PEACEMAKER

The cities in Italy were continually at war with one another. Within the cities factions quarreled with each other over land, social standing, and competitive advantages in trade.

Francis and his brothers as individuals and as a community presented themselves as an antidote to this habit of war. They were men from different social backgrounds living together in peace. They were not identified with powerful members of the landed clergy; they were not seen as carrying out a clerical agenda. Therefore they came to be trusted mediators who helped to settle conflicts between hostile individuals and communities.

Francis wanted to create a "culture of peace" that all could follow based on their values and their duties to God and neighbor. He did so by first reminding his listeners of the fundamental relationship between peace and penance. Each person must begin by finding peace within, which subjugates evil impulses to the life of the Spirit. Only after the penitent is restored to the divine order that has been disrupted by sin can one seek peace in this world. Lasting peace depends on the continued goodwill to establish, restore, and maintain it. [39]

Late in life Francis heard of the conflict between the Podesta (civil chief magistrate) of Assisi, Don Oportulo, and Bishop Guido. It is unclear what the issue was, but it was serious enough for Bishop Guido to excommunicate the podesta. This news of civil discord added to Francis' physical suffering, as he lay near death in the middle of a bitter winter.

Francis' response was to add a stanza to his canticle, praising those who, like Christ on the cross, forgave their enemies and lived in peace.

> Blessed be you, my Lord, through
> those who give pardon for your Love,
> and who bear infirmity and tribulation.
>
> Blessed are those who endure in peace for by you,
> Most High, shall they be crowned. [40]

Francis arranged for Don Oportulo and his staff to assemble before the bishop's palace. The expectation was that Francis would come, or send his emissaries, to arbitrate the issue. Instead, he sent two brothers to sing the canticle in the presence of all concerned, with the new stanza blessing those who were committed to peace.

> The podesta was so affected by the gesture that he rose, announced that he was withdrawing his grievances, and fell prostrate at the bishop's feet, asking forgiveness. The prelate had no choice but to ask forgiveness in turn. They embraced and exchanged the kiss of peace that, to the common mind and also at law, signified the end of a feud. [41]

Through his "Canticle of the Sun" Francis expressed the desire that peace be extended not simply in human relationships, but through all of God's creation. When the human family finally seeks ultimate peace, it recognizes that this extends beyond individual desires and fears. Finally, believers will recognize that "peacemaking does not become an activity that one does out of kindness or sympathy, but becomes a mode of acting that is part and parcel of what it means to be a follower of Christ and a believer in a God who is love." [42]

QUESTIONS

According to Saint Francis, where in the world can we truly find God?

What was Francis' advice to his friars when he sent them out to preach?

Why was Francis impatient with sad faces?

What did the people take away after they experienced a sermon from Saint Francis?

According to Saint Francis, what are the steps we can take to bring about a culture of peace?

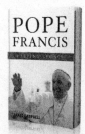

Pope Francis: A Living Legacy
Share this book with your family and friends!

Request 6 copies for $18 online at **www.DynamicCatholic.com**

CHAPTER 4

IGNATIUS' WORLD

In the 265 years between the death of Francis of Assisi and the birth of Ignatius Loyola, there were many changes in the Mediterranean world, and still many similarities. There were still hostile relations between a growing Islamic world in the eastern Mediterranean and North Africa and the Western kingdoms. The Western kingdoms had begun to expand down the coast of Africa and across the Atlantic Ocean to discover what were for them new lands and new opportunities for wealth. Saint Francis had lived at a time when the Church was flourishing with the building of Gothic cathedrals, the growth of religious communities, and the expansion of trade. In the time between Saint Francis and Ignatius, Western Europe had suffered an epidemic of bubonic plague, the Black Death, most severe from 1347 to 1351. The papacy lost prestige and came under the influence of the French monarchy, moving to Avignon, France, between 1309 and 1378. This was followed by the Western Schism from 1378 to 1417, in which there were two and then three popes claiming the Chair of Saint Peter. By the end of the 1400s it was clear that the Church was in need of reform; it became a crisis after Martin Luther's posting of his 95 Theses in 1517, in reaction to the sale of indulgences in Germany. These would be among the difficulties Ignatius and his companions would need to address. As Ignatius responded to the challenges of his time, he created the foundational spirituality for the Jesuits that is the basis for the spirituality of Pope Francis.

Ignatius Loyola was born in 1491 into a noble family and a world of wonder, exploration, exploitation, war, chivalry, and religious conflict. He would first seek military glory, and then only the glory of serving Jesus Christ.

IGNATIUS' WORLD

Ignatius was born a year before Columbus discovered the Americas in 1492. Columbus' adventure into the west was part of a greater story of exploration from the Iberian Peninsula. When Ignatius was six, in 1498, Vasco da Gama, sailing from Portugal around the Horn of Africa and across the Indian Ocean, made landfall in India. This opened new trade routes for Christian nations to tap the sources of the spice trade and its immense profits.

In 1513, when Ignatius was twenty-two, Vasco Núñez de Balboa crossed the Isthmus of Panama to be the first European to see the Pacific Ocean. Ignatius' older brother Hernando died on that expedition.

Expeditions in the west to Central America, Mexico, and South America led Spanish adventurers to strip indigenous civilizations of their wealth and tap into the rich silver and gold mines of the New World. In 1519 Hernán Cortés led a small army of five hundred men into Mexico. With the help of native allies, he marched on Tenochtitlán, the Aztec capital and home to ruler Montezuma II. After some initial setbacks, Cortés finally took the city, stripping it of its gold and jewels, which he sent back to Spain.

Reading about Cortés' adventures inspired his distant cousin Francisco Pizarro to take an expedition to the west coast of South America. By 1535 he had conquered the Inca Empire, founded the city of Lima, Peru, and exploited the native labor that had not died from the smallpox epidemic transmitted by the Europeans, making them work in the fabulously rich silver mines.

These discoveries and many others stoked the fires of ambition of young men in Spain who saw the whole world opening up to fulfill their dreams of glory and riches.

THE AGE OF PRINT

In 1452 Johannes Gutenberg began a three-year process of printing a two-volume edition of the Bible using a technique of movable type on a printing press. By 1455 he had produced two hundred copies of his beautiful Bible. More important, the means by which he had produced the Bible revolutionized the communication of ideas in Europe. Gutenberg failed in keeping his process secret, and by 1500 some twenty-five hundred European cities had established printing presses.

Gutenberg's printing press created the world of modern reading and scholarship. It made possible the production of multiple inexpensive editions of the Bible and the works of the fathers of the Church and of ancient philosophy. As handwritten manuscripts were brought into print, it became possible for scholars like Erasmus of Rotterdam to create a critical edition of the New Testament in 1522, which compared and corrected mistakes that were inevitable in hand-copied manuscripts.

The impact of the printing press and the (then) lightning-fast distribution of information had a direct impact on the Protestant Reformation, sparked by Martin Luther's critique of the sale of indulgences [43] in Germany in 1517. Luther, an Augustinian priest and Scripture scholar, was furious over the carnival atmosphere in which the indulgences were sold by Johann Tetzel and his group. The indulgence certificates were printed by the thousands and marketed with a ditty that went something like:

> As soon as the money in the coffer does ring
> The soul from purgatory to heaven does spring.

Martin Luther's *The Ninety-Five Theses on the Power and Efficacy of Indulgences,* with its critique of indulgences and other clerical abuses, immediately went to print. Within two weeks of the document's release, copies had been distributed throughout Germany. Within two months they were being read throughout Europe. Soon the German princes and free cities in Northern Europe discovered that they had a common cause: the critique of the Roman Catholic Church. There was little charity in the attempts at communication between Luther and his supporters and the representatives of the Catholic Church. This led first to schism, then to a complete break with Roman Catholicism.

While the printing press had facilitated dissension in Germany, it also made it possible for spiritual classics to be more widely read among the Catholic laity. Now Ignatius and other literate men and women of his generation could read works of Christian spirituality at home, rather than going to a monastery or cathedral chapel library to read hand-transcribed scrolls. Ignatius was well acquainted with the power of the printing press, purchasing one for the Jesuit community as soon as he became master general.

Today we are experiencing an even more rapid expansion of communications media. Radio, television, and especially the Internet are instantly connecting people all over the world. More and more we are witnesses to events happening on the other side of the world. Pope Francis has a keen awareness of the ability to get the message of Jesus out through the new media channels, as the world witnessed in the Vigil for Peace in Syria on September 7, 2013, which was simultaneously broadcast around the world.

INTERNAL CRISIS IN THE CHURCH

The Church that Ignatius was baptized into was in disarray and in need of serious reform. The centralized curial system was corrupt, selling ecclesial appointments, which were great cash cows for the people who bought the positions. The Curia sold them to the highest bidder. Bishops could become the ordinary in more than one diocese in order to reap the income from each of them. This can be seen especially in the career of the twenty-three-year-old Albrecht of Brandenburg, who was not only the Archbishop of Mainz but also received the financial benefits of two other bishoprics and a large number of rich abbeys. [44]

It was an arrangement with the Roman Curia on the part of Albrecht of Brandenburg that led to Martin Luther's *95 Theses*. It cost Albrecht the immense sum of ten thousand ducats to the Curia for the dispensation to be bishop of three dioceses—Mainz, Magdeburg (both archbishoprics), and Halberstadt. To pay for the dispensation, Albrecht borrowed the money from the Fugger banking firm. To recoup the money, he was given permission to have Johann Tetzel preach the indulgences, with half the proceeds going to the Fugger banking firm and half going to Albrecht. We have already seen the consequences of this deal in Luther's protest.

The fallout from Luther's actions, and the inept responses from Rome, led to the most severe crisis in the Church's history.

But it would hardly be an exaggeration to say that Luther's revolt was the most devastating of them all. Never before was there so widespread and sudden a desertion of its altars, and never before had so many priests and nuns abandoned their cloisters, almost overnight. When it was all over, half of Europe was lost to the Roman obedience, and the unity of Christendom was but a fading memory. [45]

It would be a major task of the early Jesuit community, founded by Ignatius Loyola, to proclaim the Gospel and save for the Church many communities otherwise lost to the protesters.

The efforts of Ignatius and the other early Jesuits were among those of a growing number of Catholic reformers seeking to bring a revitalized Catholic spirituality back into the Church. Among the early reform movements seeking to re-center the Church on the path to holiness were a number of German bishops who had begun renewal efforts in their dioceses. Their endeavors made the situation brought about by Tetzel's antics all the more embarrassing.

There were also lay-inspired reform movements—like the Oratory of Divine Love, founded in Genoa in about 1499—in which the members sought personal sanctity by means of good works on behalf of others. [46]

But the strongest reform movement was taking place in Spain under the leadership of Jiménes de Cisneros, Archbishop of Toledo (d. 1517).

His new University of Alcalá he made a seminary of bishops and a center of humanistic studies that fused the new learning and the old theology in an original synthesis. Under men like [Jiménes] the King and clergy learned how to collaborate without detriment to the authority of either in a program that combined reform with respect for tradition. It is no accident that Spain provided the leaders of the extraordinary Catholic Reformation that swept the whole Church after the Council of Trent. [47]

Finally, Ignatius and his early companions were educated in the age of humanistic studies of the Renaissance. He met his first companions at the University of Paris, where they were all working on master's degrees. After they completed their education and failed to get to the Holy Land, they settled in Rome, pledging their services to the pope. In the humanism of the Italian Renaissance that they had learned in Paris, they learned and practiced the Ciceronian ideal of living happy and virtuous lives in this world. In this atmosphere they cultivated the values of strong membership in a community, but also of individual expression.

> But there was also a new sense of being an individual, a *uomo singulare*, with feelings and opinions worthy of expression. The newly invented sonnet form of poetry encouraged the expression of inward personal experience. Biography and portrait painting, though neither was a new genre, thrived as never before. As voyagers and geographers explored and described newly discovered peculiarities about the outside world, humanist authors explored and described the peculiarities of the human condition. [48]

The early Jesuits would take these humanistic ideals with them into the schools they established.

The principle that grace builds on nature lies at the heart of Ignatian humanism. Without that principle—

or something akin to it—there can be no spiritual or religious humanism, Christian or otherwise. Believing in the affinity between creation and grace explains why the church fathers could borrow freely from the categories and insights of pagan Greek and Roman authors. It explains why Dante could revere Virgil and why Petrarch wished he could count Cicero a Christian. Individuals first have to affirm the possibility of truth outside their own community before they can look and learn outside of it. On the basis of that Thomistic principle, Jesuits would insist on teaching "pagan" classics and resist all efforts to oppose it. [49]

CONCLUSION

So into an age of a Church in need of reform, an ever-increasing educated population with access to printed books and needing articulate preachers and teachers in an expanding world of conquest and slaughter, came a small man walking on a gimpy leg with his heart ablaze with the love of Jesus. How did God call him on this mission?

QUESTIONS

In what way was the world Ignatius was born into becoming dynamically different than that of Saint Francis?

How did actions and attitudes within the Church contribute to the success of Luther's protests?

What was an important difference between the early Franciscan Friars and the early Jesuits?

What is the importance of the principle of "grace builds on nature"?

CHAPTER 5

FROM COURTIER TO NEW LIFE

Ignatius Loyola (baptized Iñigo Lopez) was born the youngest of thirteen into a Basque noble family of great lineage in service to the crown. His father was next to the king in battle at the siege of Granada (1482–1492), the last Muslim state on the Iberian Peninsula. His oldest brother, Juan Pérez, was killed in battle at Naples when Ignatius was five years old. As we have seen, another older brother, Hernando, died in the Isthmus of Panama on the expedition with Balboa. Another of Ignatius' brothers, whose name is lost, died fighting the Turks in Hungary. Ignatius' early years were filled with stories of great battles and heroic travels that would fill his imagination the rest of his life. [50]

According to the laws of the time, the oldest son received the inheritance and title, while the younger sons had to find their own way in the world. As the youngest family member, Ignatius would have been destined by his family for a clerical career, and he received tonsure as a boy as a first step in that direction. However, he must have impressed his father with his worldly ambition. When the royal treasurer, Don Juan Velázquez de Cuéllar, high steward for the Catholic Majesties, invited Ignatius' father to send a son to be a page in his court, he sent Ignatius. [51]

IGNATIUS AS COURTIER

Ignatius thoroughly enjoyed his years in court. There he learned the skills of dance, music, and poetry. He was imbued with a spirit of chivalry, learning the practice of making war, the skills of being a courtier. He also filled his head with the classic romances, with their visions of conquest and glory, for which he was ready to endure hardship and sacrifice. These were the images the conquistadores Cortés and Pizarro remembered as they traveled through the forests, swamps, and mountains of the Americas.

As a member of the court and an attractive young man, with long blond hair, Ignatius had great success with the ladies. He also had the prickly sense of honor of a young knight, given to dueling at the slightest excuse.

With the dueling came a tendency to brawl. There is a record of an incident in 1515, when Ignatius was brought before a local court for disturbing the peace.

> Iñigo was the gang leader. It took place on a carnival day, Shrove Tuesday, in February 1515. Iñigo's crimes were said to be heinous, premeditated and committed at night. It was a violent clash set off by a well laid ambush. The judge in the case described Iñigo as bold and defiant, cunning, violent and vindictive. He was armed with sword, dagger, pistol, breastplate and leather cuirass and trousers. Although his accoutrements and his long hair flowing under his velvet cap constituted a violation of canon law, he was able to invoke his status as a tonsured cleric and have the judgment referred to the Bishop of Pamplona, thus escaping civil proceedings. [52]

In 1517 Ignatius lost his patron, who was dismissed from his duties by the new King of Spain, Charles V. The patron died that same year, but his widow gave Ignatius two horses and a sum of money in gratitude for his service. Ignatius then entered the service of Don Antonio Manrique de Lara, Viceroy of Navarre. In 1521 this brought him north to Pamplona, close to the border of France.

PAMPLONA

The city of Pamplona was a pawn in the incessant wars between France and Spain. It was captured and recaptured many times, and the population simply did its best to endure the occupation until the next army came through.

In 1521 the French came to invade once again. They were at war with Charles V on many fronts, including Italy. Unable to be strong everywhere, the Spanish forces were weak in Navarre, with three thousand undisciplined troops and only seven hundred horse. The French came with an army of twelve thousand infantry, eight hundred lancers, and twenty-nine pieces of artillery. [53]

The city quickly surrendered, with Ignatius and a number of soldiers retreating to the citadel. Using his considerable talents of persuasion, Ignatius convinced everyone that they should hold out against the French.

The first French assault on the citadel failed, and the opposing forces settled for an artillery duel lasting for six hours. "The walls were finally breached but Iñigo fought on courageously until he was struck by a shot that passed between his legs shattering the right one and leaving gaping flesh wounds in the left. There was no more fighting." [54]

Ignatius was fortunate not to have had the shattered leg amputated. The treatment for amputation at the time included cauterizing the stump with white-hot irons. He was treated well by the French, who set his right leg and dressed the wounds on the left. In return Ignatius gave his shield, corselet, and dagger to the French soldiers who had assisted him. He was then taken home to the castle of Loyola, where he was welcomed by his sister-in-law, Magdalena de Araoz.

THE COURAGE OF IGNATIUS

When Ignatius had settled in, the local doctors had a chance to examine his leg. They determined that the initial setting of his broken limb had failed and the leg had to be set once again. As Ignatius tells the story speaking in the third person:

> There, with him being in a very bad state and calling doctors and surgeons from many quarters, they judged that the leg had to be pulled apart again and the bones set in their places again, saying that, because they had been badly set on the other occasion or because they had become dislocated on the journey, they were out of place and in this state it couldn't heal. And this butchery was done again, during which, just as during all the others he had previously undergone and later underwent, he never spoke a word, nor showed any sign of pain other than clenching his fists tightly. [55]

This operation was followed by a period of high fever, during which the doctors were convinced Ignatius would die. He was given the last sacraments and told that unless his fever broke that night, all would be lost. The fever did break that night, and Ignatius' condition improved until he was considered out of danger of death.

But the way the bones were healing offended Ignatius' self-image. One of the bones stuck out over the other, leaving his leg shorter, with the offending bone protruding and disfiguring his leg. He could not tolerate this. How could he return to court looking like that? So Ignatius asked the doctors whether the bone could be cut, to rid him of the unsightly bulge.

> They said that it certainly could be cut, but that the pain would be greater than all those he had undergone before, given it was now healed and it would need time to cut it. And still he decided to make a martyr of himself out of self-will, though his elder brother was horrified and was saying that such pain he himself wouldn't dare suffer. The injured man suffered it with his usual forbearance. [56]

Once the leg was cut, it was not the end of the pain, for the bone was now too short; they had to stretch it every day with appliances so Ignatius would not walk with a severe limp. He was confined to bed while the bones healed. It was at this time he asked for books to read, to overcome his boredom.

THE PRINT CULTURE AND IGNATIUS

The age of print also had a direct impact on the life of Ignatius Loyola. After his wounds were treated, he was bedridden in his brother's castle for nine months of recuperation. He was absolutely bored and asked for the latest romance novels to read, his favorite leisure reading when he was a courtier. But the only available books were a life of Christ and the lives of the saints.

These books had been brought to the castle of Loyola by Magdalena de Araoz, a former lady-in-waiting to Queen Isabella of Spain. The books were quite expensive and therefore a considerable investment on the part of her family. One was *Life of Christ,* by a Carthusian monk, Ludolph of Saxony. The original Latin work had been translated into Spanish and printed in Alcalá in four volumes from 1502 to 1503. The second work was *Lives of the Saints,* by an Italian Dominican, Jacopo de Voragine, who had died in 1298. The lives of the heroic saints were the first to appeal to Ignatius, who understood what it meant to follow a dream. [57]

The books reinforced in Ignatius an introspective spirituality. He did not simply read the books once and put them aside; he read and reread them. He filled up a personal notebook with quotes from both books and carried it with him when he journeyed. He would read for a while, and then set the book aside to reflect on what he had read. These periods of continued reflection helped Ignatius discover the life that God was calling him to. These were also the beginning steps of his eventual composition of *The Spiritual Exercises,* his classic work of spiritual companionship.

We see here one difference between the spiritual journeys of Francis of Assisi and Ignatius. In comparison with the great number of letters and documents written by Ignatius, Francis wrote little. He was a preacher who vibrated with enthusiasm as he acted out the story of the Gospels, bringing communities together. People were inspired by Francis as a charismatic figure who communicated in personal ways the depths of his faith.

Ignatius followed a systematic method offered to him with the stories he read and the notes he wrote down. These became the foundation for a guide in which individual souls could discover the path that God had laid out for them in this life. So the focus of Ignatius' ministry was the care of souls one at a time.

Now moving in an increasingly educated culture after his commitment to Jesus Christ, Ignatius went on to get a college degree. He was an extremely effective administrator of the early Jesuit community, and wrote more than five thousand letters over the course of his life. It was this trajectory of his journey that was facilitated and made possible by the printed word.

INSPIRED TO BECOME A SAINT

Ignatius began to be transformed by his reading of the lives of Jesus and the saints. He was first attracted to the lives of the saints, men who followed their dreams. He was challenged by the lives of Saint Francis of Assisi and Saint Dominic. He began to think there was nothing they had accomplished that he could not strive to do in his own life.

> And thus he used to think over many things which he was finding good, always proposing to himself difficult and laborious things. And as he was proposing these, it seemed to him he was finding in himself an ease as regards putting them into practice. But his whole way of thinking was to say to himself: "St Francis did this, so I must do it; St Dominic did this, so I must do it." [58]

Even so, Ignatius' dreams of glory, of impressing a special lady whom he adored from afar, did not leave him. While he spent many hours imagining what he could do to impress her, and what he would do once healed, he came away from these dreams feeling empty and tired. They no longer carried the luster they once had; instead, they made him feel vacuous and dried out.

However, when he dreamed of doing the great things Francis and Dominic had done, the results were the opposite: "But when about going to Jerusalem barefoot, and about not eating except herbs, and about doing all the other rigors he was seeing the saints had done, not only used he to be consoled while in such thoughts, but he would remain content and happy even after having left them aside." [59]

It took Ignatius a while to consider what all of this meant, why one set of dreams left him dry and disenchanted and the other left him content and happy. He realized that the dreams that were so disenchanting were coming from the devil, while the dreams that were stirring him to greater accomplishments were coming from God.

> The point of no return, so to speak, occurred one night when, unable to sleep, he saw clearly before him the likeness of Our Lady and was filled with sheer happiness that lasted many hours. He was conscious of a presence that gave him a total revulsion from his old dissolute life. The experience completed his conversion. All the licentious images imprinted on his imagination were there no longer. He assigns no date to the vision but from that night to the day he dictated this page of his autobiography he was never again troubled by temptations of the flesh. [60]

However far Ignatius had come, this was but the beginning of his journey.

QUESTIONS

What was an early indication of the leadership qualities of Ignatius?

What was the role of imagination in leading Ignatius to realize his vocation?

How did Ignatius discern the direction in which God was calling him in his life?

How can we apply these same principles in our own lives?

CHAPTER 6

IGNATIUS IN SEARCH OF HIS MISSION

The next steps Ignatius took are similar to the journey of Saint Francis of Assisi. Ignatius' family could not help but notice his change in demeanor. He began to speak of spiritual things. He copied passages from the *Life of Christ,* the *Lives of the Saints,* and the Scriptures, which ultimately reached three hundred pages of personal notes.

His ambition changed—instead of returning to the royal court, he dreamed of a pilgrimage to Jerusalem. Then he dreamed of living a life of penance for his former sinful ways, eating herbs, and fasting.

Ignatius was well beloved by his family, who suspected that he was going in a new direction and expressed their concern. He kept his dreams quiet for a while. He collected a debt from the Duke of Navarre, who was more than willing to have Ignatius return to his service. He instead traveled to the monastery at Montserrat to begin a period of penance.

MONTSERRAT

When Ignatius arrived at the monastery, he first made an arrangement with a confessor to make a general confession. It took him three days to write out all that he wanted to confess.

In a manner reminiscent of Saint Francis of Assisi, Ignatius gave away the mule he had traveled on, and had his sword and dagger hung in the church at the altar of Our Lady. He then stripped himself of his knightly clothes, gave them to a poor man, and approached Our Lady in the poorest garb he could find. He made an all-night vigil before the image of Our Lady of Montserrat.

His leg was not completely healed, and he had to bandage it at night, as it swelled up during the day. In spite of the continuing pain, he fulfilled his desire to pray: "And he went to kneel before the altar of Our Lady. And sometimes in this posture, at other times standing, he spent the whole night with his staff in his hand." [61]

Ignatius left Montserrat before dawn so as not to be recognized. Instead of going to Barcelona, as he had told his family he would, he detoured to the small town of Manresa. [62]

BACKGROUND OF MANRESA

The months that Ignatius spent at Manresa shaped the direction of the rest of his life and spiritual journey. This was a period of testing, of overcoming a severe attack of scruples, in which he could not think anything but the worst of himself. So far we have looked at the bare bones of his conversion to Christ. It must also be seen in a broader context of his chivalric and Catholic heritage.

While Ignatius' years at court created the proud, tempestuous young man, they also imbued him with the vision of serving a cause larger than himself. He dreamed of doing great deeds, of changing the world. It was this habit of thought that he would refocus in terms of his goals. "In short, there began that attitude which he later transposed to the spiritual realm when he spoke of the meditation on the Kingdom of Christ about 'the man who was willing to signalize himself in every kind of service for his King and supreme Lord.'" [63]

We have seen the positive influence of Ignatius' sister-in-law, Magdalena de Araoz, who was a presence of love and grace. She brought to Loyola not only the volumes that changed Ignatius' life but also a beautiful image of the Annunciation, which is still in the chapel at Loyola, where Ignatius often prayed.

The court where Ignatius had been in service, at Arévalo, was also the center of the Franciscan spirit of reform promoted by Cardinal de Cisneros, a spirit that continued when Don Juan Velázquez de Cuéllar took his household to court.

We have looked at some of the negative consequences of Ignatius' training in court. But he also learned the positive attributes that would continue to make him such an attractive figure and leader of men.

> These particulars tell us that he never blasphemed, for to some degree he felt within himself a sense of reverence for the Divine Majesty; that he had an instinctive aversion for every form of lying and that "he was very conscientious regarding this point even then" . . . and he had a fully developed, aristocratic feeling for spiritual purity; that he was entirely free from all attachment to money and earthly possessions. [64]

In his continuing reflection on how God was calling him, Ignatius was acutely conscious of how the life of holiness God was building within him was founded on the positive virtues he had learned from his family and from his experiences in court.

MANRESA

Ignatius began his time in Manresa acting in a way Francis of Assisi would have understood. All his life he had been rather vain in his appearance, his long blond hair looking neat at all times. Now he let it grow uncombed and wild. He also let his fingernails and toenails grow, which until that time he had kept carefully manicured. He began a severe fast, not eating the food or drink offered to him. He experienced great consolations, moments when he especially felt loved and cherished by the Lord. But such moments are transient and are followed by periods of spiritual emptiness. Ignatius fell into a kind of despair during the empty periods.

He was especially attacked by scruples, rendering harsh judgments on himself, wanting to continue to confess the sins that he had already confessed at Montserrat. These attacks continued to be severe for a number of months and included the temptation to commit suicide, as he felt so hopeless in the face of these images of his sinfulness. His fasting became even more severe; he finally did not eat for a week, and only began again on the order of his confessor.

Finally, it was his experience of reading about the lives of Christ and the saints and reflecting on the difference between the dreams that came from the devil and those that came from God that brought him through this trying period.

> And since he now had some experience of the differ-
> ence in kind of spirits through the lessons God had
> given him, he began to mull over the means through
> which that spirit had come. As a result he decided, with
> great clarity, not to confess anything from the past any
> more. Thus from that day onward he remained free of

those scruples, holding it for certain that Our Lord in his mercy had willed to liberate him. [65]

Ignatius had come through that particular valley of death and made the decision to turn to a healthier lifestyle, based on his own reflection of where God was taking him on his spiritual journey.

MOVING FORWARD IN GOD

Having lived through temptation, Ignatius then experienced a series of visions that turned him from a self-centered habit of worrying about his sinful life to becoming a missionary for God.

He had a great experience of the Trinitarian presence of God in his life, making prayer to the Trinity a focus of his spirituality. He began to see how the presence of God shines through creation, which became a source of great joy for him. (At the same time he began to once again take care of his appearance.) At Mass, meditating on the Eucharistic host being raised, he had an ever more profound awareness of the presence of the Lord in the sacrament. The image of the risen Christ and Mary became more vivid in his prayer. Finally, all seemed to come together in a vision as he sat by the river Coriander.

> And as he was seated there, the eyes of his understanding began to be opened: not that he saw some vision, but understanding and knowing many things, spiritual things just as much as matters of faith and learning, and this with an enlightenment so strong that all things seemed new to him. . . . *And this left him with the understanding enlightened in so great a way that it seemed*

to him as if he were a different person, and he had another
mind, different from that which he had before. [66]

His experience of the presence of God the Creator in nature gave Ignatius a profound awareness of the glory of God in the whole universe. He learned to respect the source of the grandeur of the world in God. "Henceforth it is 'in the light of the Creator' as he says, and 'with a love that comes from above,' that he will look on all reality as animated by the divine dynamism of creation which sets its course toward God. It is 'in the light of the Creator' that he will look on the world, interpret it, love it, use it." [67]

In the months following these visions, Ignatius suffered from severe illness once more, even to the point of death, probably as a result of the extreme fasting he practiced.

All the while he continued to write in his notebook and reflect on the path that God was bringing him on. Having learned so much, he now was filled with a desire to be a companion for others on their journey with God and began to practice what became known as *The Spiritual Exercises*. "During Ignatius' sojourn at Manresa, God gave him a most profound insight into, and feeling for, the mysteries of our holy Faith and the Catholic Church. At that time also He inspired him with *The Spiritual Exercises* by moving him to devote himself entirely to the service of God and the salvation of souls." [68]

QUESTIONS

How did the values Ignatius learned as a young man exemplify the principle of grace building on nature?

Why was Ignatius' experience of scruples so potentially damaging to his spiritual development?

How did his experience of discernment help Ignatius move beyond the experience of scruples?

How did Ignatius see the relationship of creation to God after his experience at the Coriander River?

CHAPTER 7

IGNATIUS THE PILGRIM

In 1523 Ignatius decided it was time to travel to the Holy Land, where he hoped to remain for the rest of his life. He refused to take a companion, determined that he would trust God alone. In his biography Ignatius tells of the difficulties of travel, the companions he met, his willingness to beg for the food he had to bring on board the ship for his own use. From Spain he eventually arrived at Venice, where he could take a ship to the Holy Land.

When Ignatius finally arrived in Jerusalem with his fellow pilgrims, he was greeted by the Franciscan friars who were responsible for guiding them through the holy sites, leading the experiences in prayer, and keeping everyone safe and within the bounds allowed by the Muslim authorities.

During Ignatius' visit, Jerusalem was especially unsafe:

> In September a squadron of five hundred ... Turkish cavalry, violently Anti-Christian, arrived in Jerusalem from Damascus and the pilgrims were advised not to be seen in the streets. During the following days of enforced retreat Iñigo visited the local Superior of the Franciscans to seek permission to remain in the Holy Land. Perhaps it was unfortunate that his request was made while the Turkish troops were in the city. [69]

Ignatius' request was refused, but he did not want to take no for an answer. He wanted to preach to and convert the Muslims in Jerusalem, which was, as it had been in Francis of Assisi's time, a desire for a martyr's death. The Franciscans were a poor community in a fragile social environment, trying their best to stay in the background. They also had endured the ransoming of Christians, whom they were obliged to get back with their meager resources. Ignatius finally spoke to the Franciscan provincial. In his most persuasive manner he told the provincial he would stay, unless it was a manner obliging him under pain of sin.

> To this the Provincial said that they had authority from the Holy See to make anyone leave there or stay there whom they saw fit, and to be able to excommunicate anyone who was not willing to obey them. And in this case, it was their judgment that he mustn't remain etc. When he wanted to show him the bulls on the strength of which they could excommunicate him, he told them that there was no need to see them: he believed their Reverences, and since this was their judgment, with the authority they had, he would obey them. [70]

Before he left, Ignatius snuck away from the group of pilgrims to visit the Mount of Olives, which was off-limits to Christians. He bribed the guard to let him in, and remained until he was found by an angry friar, who brought him back to the monastery.

BARCELONA

On his return to Spain, after further adventures in war-ridden Italy, Ignatius returned to school. He needed to learn Latin, the language in which theology was taught. So he began his studies with boys a fraction of his age. He had a number of women friends who helped him, giving him lodging and food. He also continued to work on *The Spiritual Exercises*.

After two years in Barcelona his Latin was good enough that he could continue his studies at the university in Alcalá. While in Alcalá, and later in Salamanca, Ignatius attracted a number of young people, to whom he gave *The Spiritual Exercises*. This also attracted the attention of the clerical authorities; Ignatius spent some time imprisoned by the Inquisition. His writings were examined and considered orthodox, but he was told to receive ordination before giving the exercises again. Ignatius eventually decided to go to Paris to continue his studies.

THE SPIRITUAL EXERCISES

The Spiritual Exercises is not a manual of spirituality, but a set of notes that Ignatius began in Manresa and added to over the years. The notes are meant for the director facilitating the exercises to help the exercitant discover how God is calling him or her to a life in service to others. God is the ultimate director of the process.

Ignatius states the goal of *The Spiritual Exercises* in the First Principle and Foundation:

> The human person is created to praise, reverence and serve God Our Lord, and by so doing to save his or her soul. The other things on the face of the earth are created for human beings in order to help them pursue the end for which they are created. It follows from this that one must use other created things in so far as they help towards one's end, and free oneself from them in so far as they are obstacles to one's end. To do this we need to make ourselves indifferent to all created things, provided the matter is subject to our free choice and there is no prohibition. Thus as far as we are concerned, we should not want health more than

illness, wealth more than poverty, fame more than dis-
grace, a long life more than a short one, and similarly
for all the rest, but we should desire and choose only
what helps us more towards the end for which we are
created. [71]

The exercises are divided into four periods, called "weeks" by
Ignatius because the process is designed to last for thirty days.
In the first week the exercitant is brought face-to-face with the
history of sin and his personal participation in this life of sin.
But this is not so as to lapse into self-hatred over his actions.
The context of these reflections is realizing that in spite of all
the choices made against God, he is loving, merciful, forgiv-
ing, and patient, and wants only to have a deeper relationship
with the exercitant. (We see this as a consistent theme in Pope
Francis' homilies on the mercy and forgiveness of God.)

In the second week, with meditations on the Infancy Nar-
ratives and Jesus in the temple, the exercitant uses his imagination to enter into the life of Jesus, exploring Jesus' humanity.
The goal is to enter into a relationship with Jesus and to discover in the recognition of his humanity how God is calling the
exercitant to become more human in his own time and place.
The question is asked, Whom am I ready to serve? Will I take
up the standard of Satan and follow the values of the world,
or will I take up the standard of Christ the King in a life of
service for others?

In week three the exercitant imagines himself in the Passion
and death of Jesus Christ. Meditating on these events leads to
becoming more intensely compassionate and empathetic, recognizing that Jesus did not abandon the human family. Jesus
came to share in everything that it means to be human; thence
is the model and means by which the exercitant can become

everything of what it means to be human in his own time and place.

The fourth week is the Resurrection, recognizing that Jesus Christ is alive today. It calls the exercitant in his growth as a person to be a sign to the world of what it means to be Christ today.

In each of the concluding three points of the contemplation, Ignatius writes, "I will reflect on myself." God is present in us, working in us, self-giving in us. The Exercises end, and we return to our routines filled with a sense of divine immanence—in the world, in our lives, and in our labors, no matter how busy or mundane. The Ignatian ideal is that now we can recall and relive an experience of "union and familiarity" with God that uplifts and sustains us no matter the distractions of our work or banality of our lives. [72]

IGNATIUS' FIRST COMPANIONS

In Paris, Ignatius continued to help others. There he also found the companions who would be the founders with him of the Society of Jesus. He gave *The Spiritual Exercises* to Peter Favre, Francis Xavier, Simon Rodrigues, Diego Lainez, Alfonso Salmeron, and Nicolas Bobadilla.

Almost effortlessly he attracted high-minded students to himself. In a sophisticated society he was always unaffectedly friendly, candid and direct. As in his Exercises what he said was simple but memorable, unoriginal but striking. No matter whom he met he brought to them the awareness of another presence. The impact was perhaps all the more effective because he was not a religious by profession and was ready always to confess himself a sinner. [73]

The seven companions became a community, pronouncing personal vows on the feast of the Assumption on August 15, 1534.

IN SERVICE TO THE POPE

In 1537 the companions went to Venice to travel to the Holy Land. However, the Ottoman Turks were at war with the Venetians, cutting off their access. As they waited for clearance to travel, the companions placed themselves in service to the people they could care for in the hospitals in Venice.

> One should not confuse our contemporary idea of a hospital—all antisepsis and clean sheets—with hospitals in the sixteenth century, bereft of either anesthesia or indoor plumbing. The groaning, screams, and smells can only be imagined. Receiving no payment save their room and board, Ignatius and his companions scrubbed floors and emptied slop buckets, dug graves and prepared corpses for burial. One of their number, Simon Rodrigues, later described the experience as one of hunger and exhaustion, revulsion at their surroundings, and fear of contagion. If there is a popular image of Jesuits today, it's that of the priest-professor, an intellectual with chalk on his hands but clean fingernails. Outsiders unfamiliar with their history do not ordinarily think of Jesuits nursing victims of sexually transmitted disease. But long before taking charge of classrooms, they were involved in any number of such tasks guaranteed to get their hands dirty. [74]

With the access to the Holy Land cut off, the companions went to Rome to place themselves in service to the pope. In Rome they taught theology, preached in the market squares, catechized the young, heard confessions, worked in the hospitals. They showed God's love more in deeds than in words. After a year of examination and controversy, Pope Paul II gave formal approval for the Society of Jesus on September 27, 1540.

CONCLUSION

One cannot help but see the similarities in the stories of Francis of Assisi and Ignatius. Both came from families who were well off—Francis from a merchant's family; Ignatius from Basque aristocracy. Both valued the ideals of chivalry and were generous to others. Ignatius became a knight who found glory in battle, a place of honor that Francis could only aspire to. When God called them to service, their first reaction was to express deep sorrow for their sins and practice stringent forms of penance that would permanently harm their health. Both men discovered the joy of recognizing the presence of God suffusing all of creation.

Francis of Assisi's enduring legacy is his concern for the poor and marginalized, his celebration of the presence of God in nature, and his passion for peace, not only among neighbors, but among all who live.

Ignatius gave us through his teaching and example the same generosity toward others that we find in Francis of Assisi. He also gave to us *The Spiritual Exercises*, a reliable set of principles that anyone can follow to explore the depths of God's love and the direction God is calling them in service to others.

In his lifestyle Pope Francis follows the example of Francis of Assisi in letting go of or not taking on any of the trappings of whatever office he has held, so his energy can be in support of all, especially the poor.

As a faithful member of the Society of Jesus, Pope Francis is well known as a profoundly loving director of *The Spiritual Exercises* who has a passion for helping others discover the loving and forgiving God who has so deeply molded his heart.

QUESTIONS

When we read Ignatius' First Principle and Foundation, how does our conception of Christian life compare to this principle?

When we think of human sinfulness, does it lead us to discouragement or to a greater sense of the mercy of our loving Father?

How ready are we to use our imagination to create opportunities for personal conversations with Jesus Christ?

How well do we appreciate the presence of God in our everyday life and experiences?

CHAPTER 8

PREPARATION FOR A PAPAL MINISTRY

The 444 years between the death of Saint Ignatius Loyola and the year 2000 saw the rise and fall of empires, the colonization of the world by Western Europe, and in the late twentieth century the loss of those colonies. The communications revolution that began in the early twentieth century with radio and grew to include television and the Internet has made our civilization one of instant awareness of events around the world. The globalization of the economy has created a new set of winners and losers—those in a position to take advantage of the new economic stage, and those increasingly being left behind.

Having come from Argentina and belonging to the Bishops of Latin America and the Caribbean, Pope Francis brings a particular sensitivity to the economic and social issues of globalization and its impact on the poor. He has also shown himself to be a quick learner, using the means of modern communication to proclaim the message of Jesus to a wounded world. His role as head of the Bishops of Latin America and the Caribbean prepared him for his papal ministry.

FIFTH CONFERENCE OF LATIN AMERICAN AND CARIBBEAN BISHOPS

In 2007 Pope Benedict XVI attended the Fifth General Conference of the Bishops of Latin America and the Caribbean, in Aparecida, Brazil. At the conference the future pope, Cardinal Jorge Mario Bergoglio, was overwhelmingly chosen from among the 130 bishops to chair the committee to write the final report. This document was written to lay out the goals of the conference for the next ten years. Those who participated in the study groups in preparation for the report said that Bergoglio was a patient and open facilitator of the process. He encouraged all to be open to the Holy Spirit and conscious of the presence of the risen Jesus Christ among them, guiding their work.

The Concluding Document: Fifth General Conference of the Bishops of Latin America and the Caribbean was presented to Pope Benedict XVI. On June 29, 2007, the Solemnity of Saints Peter and Paul, Pope Benedict XVI authorized the publication of the concluding document, now known as *The Aparecida Document.*

The first part of *The Aparecida Document* describes the social, cultural, political, ethnic, and ecological situation in Latin America. In the present-day world of increasing globalization and instant communication, it is clear that the issues discussed in the document are those that affect us all.

BEING CATHOLIC TODAY

Early in *The Aparecida Document* the conference notes some of the limitations in the practice of the Catholic faith today. It laments a Catholic faith that is part of someone's everyday baggage, a collection of rules and prohibitions, fragmented devotional practices, and a cafeteria kind of selection of and partial adherence to the truths of the faith. Some sacraments are only occasionally practiced, doctrinal principles are repeated without true understanding, and there is a tendency to fall into bland or nervous moralizing. The bishops believe that the practice of the Catholic faith on this level will never survive the challenges of an increasingly secularized world. [75]

What is lacking in this practice of Catholicism, according to the bishops, is the recognition that being Christian is an encounter with the person of Jesus Christ.

> Here lies the fundamental challenge that we face: to show the Church's capacity to promote and form disciples and missionaries who respond to the calling received and to communicate everywhere, in an outpouring of gratitude and joy, the gift of the encounter with Jesus Christ. We have no other treasure but that. We have no other happiness, no other priority, but to be instruments of the Spirit of God, as Church, so that Jesus Christ may be known, followed, loved, adored, announced, and communicated to all, despite difficulties and resistances. This is the best service—his service—that the Church has to offer people and nations.[76]

CONSEQUENCES OF GLOBALIZATION

The Aparecida Document continues to discuss the challenges that the Church faces in the twenty-first century. The first is the dizzying effects of the development of instant communication through the media, especially the Internet. Information that one would formerly spend hours looking for in a research library is now immediately available with the push of a computer key. Television signals transmitted by satellite allow us to witness events, happy and tragic, from any place on earth as they are happening. Dedicated websites open to us the latest news in science, politics, and the humanities, but also the volatile views of extreme groups who spread messages of hate and division.

It frequently happens that some want to look at reality one-sidedly based on economic information, others on political or scientific information, others on entertainment and spectacle. However, none of these partial criteria can provide us with a coherent meaning for everything that exists. When people perceive this fragmentation and limitation, they tend to feel frustrated, anxious, and anguished. Social reality turns out to be too big for an individual mind that, aware of its lack of knowledge and information, easily regards itself as insignificant, with no real impact on events, even when adding its voice to other voices that seek one another for mutual aid. [77]

CULTURAL CONSEQUENCES

One of the consequences for all societies in this fragmenting world of information is the glorification of individual rights as the primary value. There is a lost sense of looking for the common good in political and social environments, eroding the value of community bonds. What is promoted is the creation of new and often arbitrary individual rights, a "hook up" culture of immediate sexual gratification, and the provisional character of commitments to religious and family life.

This culture is characterized by the self-reference of the individual, which leads to indifference toward the other, whom one does not need and for whom one does not feel responsible. There is a tendency to live day by day, with no long term designs, and no personal, family, and community attachments. Human relations are regarded as consumption goods, leading to emotional relations without responsible and final commitment. [78]

ECONOMIC CONSEQUENCES
OF GLOBALIZATION

There are many benefits to the globalization of the economy. Regional economies have been able to access new technologies, markets, and financing. The ideal of uniting the human family across borders seems to become more possible through interaction in the electronic community. But the positive aspects of globalization have to be seen in the context of its negative human consequences.

> In globalization, market forces easily absolutize efficacy and productivity as values regulating all human relations. This peculiar character makes globalization a process that fosters many inequalities and injustices. In its current form, globalization is incapable of interpreting and reacting in response to objective values that transcend the market and that constitute what is most important in human life—truth, justice, love, and most especially, the dignity and rights of all, even those not included in the market. [79]

What concerns the bishops in this economic environment is that while those who have access to education and technical skills can flourish in a globalized world, the poor are even more and disproportionately left behind. This especially includes the poverty of knowledge and the use of and access to the new technologies, which ultimately leads to a poverty of exclusion, making the poor susceptible to exploitation as surplus and disposable labor.

OTHER SOCIAL CONSEQUENCES

Among the most important consequences of extreme poverty is the brutal exploitation of those who are most vulnerable. This leads to many working in economic conditions of what amounts to slavery. It also leads to human trafficking and prostitution, especially of minors.

As Archbishop of Buenos Aires, Cardinal Jorge Bergoglio was especially concerned and spoke out against human trafficking. But it is not just a problem in Argentina; it is worldwide. As Michele A. Clark reports:

> Sasha is one of an estimated 2 to 4 million women and girls who are globally trafficked for purposes of commercial sexual exploitation and forced labor every year. Along with growing trade and effortless world travel, globalization has also ushered in an increase in the trafficking of human flesh. The problem is so extensive that every country in the world can be considered a country of origin, transit or destination. Primary countries of demand include Western Europe, North America and parts of the Middle East and Southeast Asia. [80]

THE GROWTH OF VIOLENCE

The social dislocation of globalization and the loss of stability and economic opportunities have reinforced a culture of violence.

> Violence takes on various forms and has different agents: organized crime and drug trafficking, paramilitary groups, common crime, especially in the outskirts of large cities, violence of youth gangs, and

growing domestic violence. The causes are many: worship of money, the advance of an individualistic and utilitarian ideology, disrespect for the dignity of each person, a deterioration of the social fabric, corruption even of law-enforcement entities, and lack of government policies on social justice. [81]

ECOLOGICAL ISSUES

Finally, Latin American and Caribbean bishops are sensitive to the budding disaster in the world's most important ecosystem. They note that preserving the environment is too often subordinated to economic development, with the consequences being the waste of water resources, air pollution, and climate change. These consequences are not just local; they are worldwide.

Latin America has the most abundant aquifers on the planet, along with vast extensions of forest lands which are humanity's lungs. The world thus receives free of charge environmental services, benefits that are not recognized economically. The region is affected by the warming of the earth and climate change caused primarily by the unsustainable way of life of industrialized countries. [82]

CONCLUSION

Pope Francis is entering his papal ministry having studied and reflected on for decades the social, environmental, political, and religious challenges that the Church faces in the twenty-first century. As we will see, he is not only conversant in the theoretical discussion of the issues but has also ministered year after year to the poor and marginalized in society, personally learning their difficulties, hopes, and dreams. In this respect, he can be seen as being very well prepared to address the needs of the world today.

QUESTIONS

What particular concerns do the bishops of Latin America and the Caribbean express about the state of Catholicism today?

What are some of the negative consequences of the speed of communication in new media?

How do the bishops describe the consequences of globalization on the life of those who are poor?

Why are the bishops so concerned about human trafficking?

What dangers do the bishops see in the destruction of the forests in the Amazon basin, which are "humanity's lungs"?

CHAPTER 9

JORGE BERGOGLIO

On December 17, 1936, Jorge Mario Bergoglio was born in Buenos Aires, Argentina. He was the first child of Mario Bergoglio and Regina Sivori Bergoglio. Jorge's father had immigrated to Argentina in 1929 to escape the grip of fascism in Italy. When he and his family arrived they were welcomed by family members who had immigrated earlier.

The Bergoglio family in Argentina was doing quite well, running a paving firm in Buenos Aires. For a time Mario worked for the firm, until it went out of business in the economic downturn of 1932. He got a job at another company, and the family started over. Jorge and his four siblings were raised in a loving family, with their basic needs provided for.

In the Bergoglio home, Sundays were sacred time. The family always went to Sunday Mass, and then had long lunches in the afternoon. The pope's sister María Elena explained:

> Those never-ending and very beautiful lunches with five, six, even seven courses. And with dessert. We were poor but with great dignity, and always faithful to what was for us the Italian tradition. Mother was an exceptional cook. She made fresh pasta, cappelletti and ragù, risotto piemontese, and delicious baked chicken. She always said that when she married Papa she didn't even know how to make a fried egg. Then our nonna Rosa, who fled Piedmont in 1929, taught her the tricks. [83]

ROSA MARGHERITA
VASALLO BERGOGLIO

Jorge's grandmother Rosa was the hero in the family. Before she left Italy in 1929 she had taken the pulpit in her local church to condemn the dictatorship of Mussolini and fascism.

Grandmother Rosa was the most important religious influence for Jorge as he grew up. She was a font of practical religious wisdom and insight on what was truly important in life. When observing a funeral she would tell her grandchildren, "A shroud has no pockets." [84]

Jorge and his siblings were close to their grandmother, spending part of each day with her. She taught Jorge to pray and told him stories of the saints, leaving a deep spiritual imprint on his life. When he was in the seminary, Rosa told him, "'Don't ever forget that you are about to become a priest and celebrating mass is the most important thing for a priest.' [Rosa] told me about a mother who told her son—a truly saintly priest—'Celebrate mass, every mass, as if it were your first and last.'" [85]

Jorge keeps two letters from Grandma Rosa in his Breviary. On the day of his ordination she wrote: "On this beautiful day on which you hold Christ our Savior in your consecrated hands and on which a wide path leading to a deeply held vocation opens up before you, I bequeath to you this humble gift of little material, but great spiritual, value." [86]

Jorge also carries a copy of a creed that she wrote for each of her grandchildren, which says in part:

> May these, my grandchildren, to whom I gave the best
> my heart has to offer, lead long and happy lives, but
> if one day hardship, illness, or the loss of a loved one
> should fill them with grief, may they remember that

one sigh directed to the tabernacle, home to the greatest and most august martyr, and a glance toward Mary at the foot of the cross, may cause a soothing drop to fall on the deepest and most painful of wounds. [87]

DISCOVERING HIS VOCATION

After Jorge had finished primary school, his father told him that he needed to find work. While the family was not well off, neither were they lacking in the basic needs, but learning to work would help Jorge grow into a more mature man. So he combined work with secondary school, getting a job in a sock factory, doing cleaning and, later, administrative work. In his fourth year of secondary school he began to specialize in food chemistry at an industrial institute, working in a lab from seven in the morning until one in the afternoon. After an hour for lunch, he went to class until late in the evening.

A great person who influenced his life at this time was his boss at the lab, Esther Balestrino de Careaga, who taught him to do the job right and to take care of the details. She was a communist sympathizer whose son and daughter-in-law had been abducted during the dictatorship in Argentina. Then she was herself abducted with two French nuns and assassinated. Jorge loved her very much and learned how to take his work seriously from her: "I truly owe much to this great woman." [88]

In all respects Jorge was a typical young man. He worked and studied, had many friends, enjoyed dancing, and was attracted to a girl he'd met in Catholic Action. That changed when he was sixteen years old.

On September 21, 1953, Jorge was planning a holiday outing with his friends. He visited his parish church and met a priest he had not seen before. He decided to celebrate the sacrament of reconciliation, and it changed his life.

> Something strange happened to me in that confession. I don't know what it was, but it changed my life. I think it surprised me, caught me with my guard down," he recalls more than half a century later. Bergoglio now has his own theory about that mystery: "It was the surprise, the astonishment of a chance encounter," he says. "I realized that they were waiting for me. That is the religious experience: the astonishment of meeting someone who has been waiting for you all along. From that moment on, for me, God is the One who *te primerea*—'springs it on you.' You search for Him, but He searches for you first. You want to find Him, but He finds you first. [89]

When he left the church, Jorge went home instead of meeting his friends. He was now convinced that God was calling him to be a priest. He did not announce this at the time, but went on to finish his schooling. At the age of twenty-one he decided to enter the seminary.

AN EXPERIENCE OF PAIN

Before he could begin his studies, Jorge went through a period of extreme pain and suffering. He had periods of high fever and pains in his chest, which it took a while to diagnose. Despite repeated visits to the hospital, the pain would not go away. He finally found spiritual comfort in his distress from a nun, Sr. Delores, a longtime acquaintance who had helped prepare him for Holy Communion. She told Jorge that in his suffering he was imitating Jesus.

The doctors finally diagnosed Jorge with a bout of serious pneumonia, and three cysts were discovered on his lungs. He underwent surgery and the upper part of his right lung was removed. His suffering continued in the weeks of convalescence as his mother had to periodically drain the fluid that accumulated in his lung.

> Jorge has lived with the physical limitations of this experience, but it also taught him how to accept the fact of pain in human life in a Christian way.

> "Pain is not a virtue in itself, but you can be virtuous in the way you bear it. Our life's vocation is fulfillment and happiness, and pain is a limitation in that search. Therefore, one fully understands the meaning of pain through the pain of God made Christ." [90]

A JESUIT VOCATION

Knowing he had a vocation to become a priest, Bergoglio initially was not clear whether he had been called to be a diocesan priest or to join a religious community. After studying at the diocesan seminary for a time, he decided to become a Jesuit. He was attracted to the Jesuits because he liked their discipline, the fact that they were on the front lines of the Church.

> It was also due to its focus on missionary work. I later had an urge to become a missionary in Japan, where Jesuits have carried out important work for many years. But due to the severe health issues I'd had since my youth, I wasn't allowed. I guess some people would have been "saved" from me here if I had been sent over there, right? [91]

Bergoglio's life as a Jesuit was customarily one of study and teaching. On March 12, 1960, he took his first vows as a Jesuit. His studies were woven in with teaching until 1969, when he was ordained a priest. He took his final vows as a Jesuit in 1973.

The most difficult years in Bergoglio's Jesuit life were undoubtedly when he was the provincial of the Jesuits in Argentina. These were approximately the same years of the brutal dictatorship of Jorge Rafael Videla Redondo, from 1976 to 1981: "His regime was marked by the systematic violation of human rights, including the torture and assassination of thousands of persons. These were the *desaparecidos,* individuals—both men and women—considered opponents of the regime, who, along with their families, were abducted and then killed." [92]

There were two Jesuit priests who were arrested, and Bergoglio was falsely accused of conspiring against them. Later investigations proved that these allegations were false, and that he had personally intervened with the dictator to have the priests released from custody. He also quietly worked as he could to hide those who were under suspicion from the government, and in one case gave his identity card to a suspect to use to leave Argentina. [93]

After leaving the position as provincial, Bergoglio continued his studies in Germany in 1986. After a time he returned to Argentina and was assigned to the University of Salvador as professor, then as confessor and spiritual director at the church of the Society of Jesus in Córdoba, Argentina.

EPISCOPAL MINISTRY

Bergoglio undoubtedly thought he would be spending the rest of his life as a confessor and spiritual director, and would have been very happy doing so. He was an excellent spiritual director, with a special gift for being a companion for those making *The Spiritual Exercises* of Saint Ignatius Loyola. But he had not gone unnoticed. Cardinal Antonio Quarracino, Archbishop of Buenos Aires, had a great appreciation for Bergoglio as a man and a priest, and the papal nuncio Monsignor Ubaldo Calabresi had regularly conferred with him on possible candidates for episcopal ordination.

So when Monsignor Calabresi called Bergoglio and asked to meet him face-to-face, Bergoglio arranged to meet him at the Córdoba airport on May 13, 1992, where Calabresi would be changing planes. After they had conversed for a while, Monsignor Calabresi was getting ready to board his flight to return to Buenos Aires.

> He asked me a range of questions on serious matters, and when the plane, which had touched down from Mendoza and was set to take off on its way back to Buenos Aires, was boarding, he told me, "Ah . . . one last thing . . . you've been named auxiliary bishop of Buenos Aires, and the appointment will be made official on the twentieth." He came out with it just like that. [95]

When asked his reaction, Bergoglio said, "My mind went blank. As I said before, my mind always goes blank after a shock, good or bad. And my initial reaction is also always wrong."

Bergoglio was auxiliary bishop of Buenos Aires for five years, and when the aging Cardinal Quarracino asked Rome for a coadjutor bishop (who would then follow him as Archbishop of Buenos Aires), Bergoglio requested that he not be transferred to another diocese, as he knew the city so well.

Then, on May 27, 2007, Bergoglio once again had lunch with Monsignor Calabresi.

> We were drinking coffee, and I was all set to thank him for the meal and take my leave when I noticed that a cake and a bottle of champagne had been brought in. I thought it must be his birthday, and I was just about to offer my best wishes. But the surprise came when I asked him about it. "No, it's not my birthday," he replied, grinning broadly. "It so happens that you are the new coadjutor bishop of Buenos Aires." [96]

Bergoglio was installed as Archbishop of Buenos Aires February 26, 1998, and on February 21, 2001, he was elevated to cardinal.

AN ARCHBISHOP AMONG THE POOR

After his installation as archbishop, Bergoglio's first decision was not to live in the elegant archbishop's residence. He took a couple of rooms for his bedroom and study, with a floor heater so as not to heat the building he resided in on weekends. He cooked for his guests, did his own dishes, and welcomed an auxiliary bishop who needed care to live with him.

Bergoglio did not have a private secretary; instead, he kept his own notes for appointments in a small notebook. He established a private line for all the priests of the archdiocese, so they could speak directly to him about any of their concerns. He did not have a car, as he preferred to travel by bus or subway, which kept him closer to the people. When he went to Rome to receive his cardinal's red hat, he appealed to his friends not to travel with him, but to donate the money to the poor. With his customary personal austerity, Bergoglio had the old wardrobe from Cardinal Quarracino tailored to meet his needs.

In all the years of his ministry as bishop and archbishop of Buenos Aires, the poor knew they had a friend in Bergoglio. He not only spoke to their needs; he went into the slums, blessed their homes, and celebrated Mass with them. He made it a special goal to provide priests to serve in the poorest slums of Buenos Aires. The priests did not just visit the neighborhoods, but lived and worked among the people. "The aim was to make the faith come alive, preaching and celebrating the sacraments while also turning the parish into a comprehensive *social service* center—fighting drugs and violence, educating the young and taking care of the old, providing job training and even community radio to give the people a voice." [97]

The work done in Villa 21, a slum of about fifty thousand people, is an example of what Bergoglio hoped would be accomplished. The Virgin of Caacupé parish runs the following ministries:

- A recovery center for drug addicts, called Lugar de Cristo

- Two farms where recovering addicts work and live

- Fifteen or sixteen chapels around the neighborhood where priests visit for Mass and confession

- A high school

- A trade school, offering courses in auto repair, electronics, laundry services, computers, and other practical job skills

- A home for the elderly

- A soup kitchen (in addition to the fact that everybody knows that if they're hanging around the parish at lunchtime, they'll probably be invited in to eat with the priests)

- A community radio station, which broadcasts 24-7 and teaches young people the media business

- A community newspaper called The Catholic

- Drug prevention programs, some targeted at paco

- A daily center for kids living in the streets, where they can get cleaned up and get a hot meal and help straightening their lives out if they want it [98]

Bergoglio did not simply send in his priests; he was constantly walking through the villas himself. Fr. José María Di Paola tells the story of inviting Bergoglio to participate in a street Mass in Villa 21–24. He set out an altar made of beer boxes and scrap wood. He had everything ready, but Bergoglio was late arriving. Fr. Di Paola could not help but worry for his safety.

The slums of Buenos Aires are known as villas miseria—villages of misery. Most residents are poor working folk. Their neighborhoods produce a shocking tally of murders each year, few of which ever get solved. For a simple measure of the profound social divide that the villas represent in Argentine society, look no further than the typical GPS device on the dashboard of local cars: They are designed to warn drivers, "Attention, you are nearing a dangerous area" if wandering too close to a villa.

There wasn't much the young priest could do that afternoon in 2000. The archbishop had insisted on coming by bus and walking, alone, to the service.

Finally, Father Di Paola spied a figure stepping matter-of-factly out of one of the ghetto's tiny brick dwellings. "You made it!" the young priest exclaimed.

The archbishop apologized for his delay. He had actually arrived early, he explained, and had decided to wander the alleys and share tugs of mate, a bitter local tea drunk from a gourd, with slum residents.

Thirteen years later, the priest still marvels at the memory. "The people were blown away," he recalls. The archbishop "was climbing up and down the alleys, blessing homes—alleys that most people from outside the villa wouldn't enter because of the danger." [99]

Bergoglio also was greatly concerned that the poor have access to the sacraments. He was severely critical of priests who would not baptize the children of unwed mothers or those of couples not married in the Church.

The child has no responsibility for the marital state of his parents. And then, the baptism of children often becomes a new beginning for parents. Usually there is a little catechesis before baptism, about an hour, then a mystagogic catechesis during the liturgy. Then, the priests and laity go to visit these families to continue with their post-baptismal pastoral care. And it often happens that parents who were not married in church maybe ask to come before the altar to celebrate the sacrament of marriage. [100]

In order to give as many people as possible the opportunity to receive the sacraments, Bergoglio made the Feast of the Immaculate Conception, on December 8, a special day for them. On that day he would celebrate a four-hour Mass in the cathedral, during which he would administer more than two hundred baptisms, four hundred confirmations, and four hundred first Communions. [101]

Along with these acts of service, Bergoglio also personally celebrated liturgies with those on the margins of society. In 2008 he celebrated the Mass of the Lord's Supper at the Hogar de Cristo, the rehabilitation center for drug addicts. As he would in the first celebration of Holy Thursday as pope, he washed the feet of twelve youths.

In his final Lenten message to the Church in Buenos Aires, on February 28, 2013, Bergoglio repeated the critique of society that was tearing his nation (and the world) apart:

> The rule of money with its devilish effects, such as drugs, corruption, trafficking in human beings—even children—together with material and moral misery: These are common currency. The destruction of dignified work, painful emigrations, and the lack of a future are also added to this symphony. Our errors and sins as the Church are not lacking in this great panorama. The most private acts of selfishness are justified, but not therefore diminished. The lack of ethical values within a society metastasizes in its families, in the life of its neighborhoods, villages, and cities; they speak to us of our limitations, our weakness, and our incapacity to transform this endless list of destructive realities. [102]

The picture that Bergoglio describes is bleak, but his message is not to give up hope:

> It is possible for everything to be new and different, because God continues to be "rich in goodness and mercy, always ready to forgive," and he encourages us to begin again and again. Today we are invited once more to undertake an Easter pathway towards life, one that includes renunciation and the Cross, one that will be uncomfortable but not fruitless. We are invited to recognize that something has gone wrong in ourselves, in society, and in the Church—to change, to make an about-face, to be converted. [103]

In 2011, at the age of seventy-five, Bergoglio submitted his resignation as Archbishop of Buenos Aires to the Vatican. He surely was looking forward to a quieter existence in which he would be able to study, pray, and continue to be a spiritual director and confessor to all who came to him. When he gave his last Lenten message, he was looking forward to celebrating the Easter Vigil with his beloved people in Buenos Aires. But the date of his Lenten message, February 28, 2013, was the last day of Pope Benedict XVI's papacy.

QUESTIONS

How does the example of Jorge Bergoglio's grandmother Rosa show the positive influence we can have on the generations that follow us?

How ready are we to be surprised by God as Bergoglio was when he was sixteen years old?

What does Bergoglio mean when he says, "Pain is not a virtue in itself, but you can be virtuous in the way you bear it"?

How did Cardinal Bergoglio's actions as bishop and archbishop of Buenos Aires hint at how he would practice his papal ministry?

What words of hope does Cardinal Bergoglio offer in his final homily in Buenos Aires?

CHAPTER 10

THE ROAD TO ROME

As bishop and as archbishop, Bergoglio focused on his ministry to the people of Buenos Aires and did not travel to Rome more than was necessary. When he became a cardinal, however, he also received assignments to committees that demanded that he travel to the Vatican more often. It is through these assignments that he became more known among his fellow cardinals and the Church in general.

The first time Cardinal Bergoglio became known to the rest of the Catholic world was in 2001. He was in Rome attending the Synod of Bishops, which was being presided over by Cardinal Edward Egan, Archbishop of New York. Cardinal Egan was called home to attend a ceremony honoring the victims of September 11, and Bergoglio took over as general counselor. He made a great impression on the bishops and received the most votes for a single bishop to join the Post-Synodal Council, representing the Americas. [105]

At the conclave in 2005, after the death of Pope John Paul II, Bergoglio was reported as the only strong candidate other than Cardinal Ratzinger in the papal election. He is said to have withdrawn his name when the votes were heading toward Ratzinger, who became Pope Benedict XVI.

Ultimately Bergoglio was elected president of the conference and chosen to lead the commission to write the final and summarizing document of the Fifth General Conference of the Bishops of Latin America and the Caribbean. He also influenced the bishops of the conference in a personal way.

> Nor was that the only recognition Bergoglio earned at that event: the day he was to give Mass, his homily elicited enthusiastic applause. No other officiating priest was applauded throughout the three weeks of the conference. Witnesses say that many of the participants took advantage of the breaks to talk with the Argentine cardinal and even take pictures with him, as if he were a famous actor or illustrious athlete. [106]

PREPARING FOR THE CONCLAVE

Pope Benedict XVI's unexpected announcement of his retirement caused "dismay, surprise, amazement and emotion" in Rome.[107] Naturally, it also began a media frenzy throughout the world. No pope had resigned since 1415, when Pope Gregory XIII stepped down to clear the way for the election of a pope who would heal the Western Schism (1378–1417).[108]

Pope Benedict's resignation took place on February 28, 2013. Beginning on March 1, the 115 cardinal electors (those cardinals under the age of eighty) from fifty countries gathered for the conclave (two eligible cardinals did not participate). On March 4, the cardinals began to meet in the general congregations to review the laws governing the voting, setting the date for the conclave. This was also the opportunity for the cardinals to discuss the key issues facing the Church.

In the general congregations the cardinals focused on four issues: the reform of the Curia, the sex abuse crisis, the needs of the global Church, and the New Evangelization. In their formal discussions at the meetings and the informal discussions during coffee breaks, the cardinals took the opportunity to get to know one another and to assess possible candidates for the papacy.

Cardinal Bergoglio had purchased a round trip ticket (flying economy, as usual) to Rome to attend the conclave. His name had not been mentioned in the majority of lists speculating about who would be elected the new pope. In general, his name was not broadly discussed among the cardinals. This apparently changed after a five-minute presentation he gave to the cardinals on one of the last days before the conclave.

Bergoglio read from a few notes during the presentation. Cardinal Jaime Ortega, Archbishop of Havana, was so impressed with the presentation that he asked Cardinal Bergoglio for a copy of his notes. After the conclave Ortega received Bergoglio's permission to publish the notes. Here is the unofficial translation from Vatican Radio, March 27, 2013.

Evangelizing Implies Apostolic Zeal

1. Evangelizing pre-supposes a desire in the Church to come out of herself. The Church is called to come out of herself and to go to the peripheries, not only geographically, but also the existential peripheries: the mystery of sin, of pain, of injustice, of ignorance and indifference to religion, of intellectual currents, and of all misery.

2. When the Church does not come out of herself to evangelize, she becomes self-referential and then gets sick. (cf. The deformed woman of the Gospel). The evils that, over time, happen in ecclesial institutions have their root in self-referentiality and a kind of theological narcissism. In Revelation, Jesus says that he is at the door and knocks. Obviously, the text refers to his

knocking from the outside in order to enter but I think about the times in which Jesus knocks from within so that we will let him come out. The self-referential Church keeps Jesus Christ within herself and does not let him out.

3. When the Church is self-referential, inadvertently, she believes she has her own light; she ceases to be the *mysterium lunae* and gives way to that very serious evil, spiritual worldliness (which according to De Lubac, is the worst evil that can befall the Church). It lives to give glory only to one another.

Put simply, there are two images of the Church: Church which evangelizes and comes out of herself, the Dei Verbum religiose audiens et fidente proclamans (these are the first words of the Vatican II Document on Divine Revelation, " Hearing the word of God with reverence and proclaiming it with faith"); and the worldly Church, living within herself, of herself, for herself. This should shed light on the possible changes and reforms which must be done for the salvation of souls.

4. Thinking of the next Pope: He must be a man who, from the contemplation and adoration of Jesus Christ, helps the Church to go out to the existential peripheries, that helps her to be the fruitful mother, who gains life from "the sweet and comforting joy of evangelizing." [109]

These five minutes impressed many cardinals, who went into the conclave with Bergoglio on their minds for the new pope. For his part, Bergoglio may have had a sense of the direction of the vote before he entered the conclave.

On the night of March 10, Fr. Thomas Rosica was walking through the Piazza Navona in Rome's historic center when he bumped into Cardinal Jorge Mario Bergoglio, whom he had known for years. Bergoglio was walking alone, wearing a simple black cassock, and he stopped and grabbed Rosica's hands.

"I want you to pray for me," the Argentine cardinal told Rosica, a Canadian priest who was assisting as a Vatican spokesman during the papal interregnum. Rosica asked him if he was nervous. "A little bit," Bergoglio said. [110]

Three days later Cardinal Bergoglio was introduced to the world as Pope Francis.

THE FIRST MONTHS

In the first months of his papacy, Pope Francis has given to the world a new encyclical, a major exhortation, homilies at major feasts and at the general audiences, and, uniquely, a treasure of homilies from the daily Mass he celebrates with Vatican employees and their families (now the assembly includes parishioners from the Archdiocese of Rome) in the chapel of the Santa Marta guesthouse. In so many ways he is proving to be a pope of surprises.

QUESTIONS

What is the implication of Cardinal Bergoglio's call for the Church to go to the peripheries?

What are the dangers for the Church of keeping Jesus Christ within herself?

What is the danger of "the worldly Church, living within herself, of herself, for herself"?

How well has Pope Francis been the kind of pope who gains life from "the sweet and comforting joy of evangelizing"?

CHAPTER 11

A POPE OF SURPRISES

Even before Pope Francis stepped out onto the balcony on the night of his election, his choice of name told the world that change was in the air. Commentators speculated about his choice; all immediately thought of Saint Francis of Assisi (which Pope Francis confirmed in his news conference the next day) and the values he represented for Christian life: the love of Lady Poverty, care of the poor and destitute, the rejection of all pomp and circumstance.

When Pope Francis came out, the world saw a quiet man in a white cassock and simple zucchetto who gave what seemed to be a shy wave to the crowd. When he spoke, it was with simple words of greeting, identifying himself as Bishop of Rome, the mother of all the churches in charity.

The world began to see the simplicity and sincerity of his actions that emulated the bearer of his chosen name. Pope Francis first asked everyone to pray for Pope Emeritus Benedict XVI. He then asked everyone if they would silently pray for him, and bowed before the people as they prayed. After the papal blessing, he left the balcony, telling the people that he hoped they would sleep well.

The next morning, Pope Francis went to the Basilica of Saint Mary Major to place flowers of devotion before the image of Mary. He chatted with the priests who would be hearing confessions during the day, emphasizing the need to assure the people confessing of God's mercy and forgiveness.

On the first Sunday after his election, Pope Francis celebrated the Eucharist at Saint Anne's parish in the Vatican without wearing papal regalia, preaching from the lectern rather than sitting in the chair, as has been the custom for the pope.

Pope Francis began his tours among the people in Saint Peter's Square, stopping the popemobile at times to pay special attention to those with disabilities. One of the first times he stopped was to greet a severely disabled man who had been brought by his family as close as they could get to the pope. As Pope Francis spoke to and blessed the man, his family thanked Pope Francis for his care and concern.

What immediately comes to mind is Mark 2:1–12, in which we see the family and friends of the paralyzed man making the effort to bring him to the roof of the house where Jesus is staying, tearing open the roof, and lowering the man so that Jesus can care for him. The faith of the family and friends, their prayers for the man who is ill, are answered by Jesus. In a similar way the prayers of family and friends for the disabled man in Rome were answered in Pope Francis' prayers of affection and blessing.

Pope Francis' care and concern for those in need continued to make international headlines when he stopped to bless and hug a young disabled girl on Easter Sunday. Since these first days the ill and the disabled have been gathering so that Pope Francis may greet each of them individually. He takes the time with everyone to listen to their story, showing each that at that moment he or she is the most important person in the world.

THREE THEMES

Pope Francis' ministry is an ever-expanding story, with new surprises, interviews, and reforms of Church practices. Following the example of his preaching, we will discuss three of the themes he has emphasized: following Jesus on the way of the cross; forgiveness, mercy, and peace; and mission to the peripheries.

CENTRALITY OF JESUS CHRIST

In his first homily to the cardinals after his election, Pope Francis described the Christian journey as that of following the crucified Jesus:

> We can walk as much as we want, we can build many things, but if we do not profess Jesus Christ, things go wrong. We may become a charitable NGO, but not the Church, the Bride of the Lord. When we are not walking, we stop moving. When we are not building on the stones, what happens? The same thing that happens to children on the beach when they build sandcastles: everything is swept away, there is no solidity. When we do not profess Jesus Christ, the saying of Léon Bloy comes to mind: "Anyone who does not pray to the Lord prays to the devil." When we do not profess Jesus Christ, we profess the worldliness of the devil, a demonic worldliness. [111]

The beginning of Pope Francis' papal ministry was in the weeks leading up to Holy Week and the celebration of the Passion, death, and Resurrection of Jesus Christ, so during his homilies, Pope Francis could focus on these central truths of the Christian faith. In his homily on Palm Sunday, he especially emphasized to the faithful the joy of the Christian following Jesus Christ.

And here the first word that I wish to say to you: joy! Do not be men and women of sadness: a Christian can never be sad! Never give way to discouragement! Ours is not a joy born of having many possessions, but from having encountered a Person: Jesus, in our midst; it is born from knowing that with him we are never alone, even at difficult moments, even when our life's journey comes up against problems and obstacles that seem insurmountable, and there are so many of them! And in this moment the enemy, the devil, comes, often disguised as an angel, and slyly speaks his word to us. Do not listen to him! Let us follow Jesus! We accompany, we follow Jesus, but above all we know that he accompanies us and carries us on his shoulders. This is our joy, this is the hope that we must bring to this world. Please do not let yourselves be robbed of hope! Do not let hope be stolen! The hope that Jesus gives us. [112]

Continuing on the themes of Holy Week and the Easter season, in his general audience on Wednesday, April 10, 2013, Pope Francis spoke on the importance of the Resurrection of Jesus Christ for all Christians who live in hope.

However, it is the Resurrection itself that opens us to greater hope, for it opens our life and the life of the world to the eternal future of God, to full happiness, to the certainty that evil, sin and death may be overcome. And this leads to living daily situations with greater trust, to facing them with courage and determination. Christ's Resurrection illuminates these everyday situations with a new light. The Resurrection of Christ is our strength! [113]

Jesus Christ is our hope and our joy. The essential truth of the Resurrection and Ascension of our Lord is that he is alive in heaven and comes to us through the Holy Spirit. Because of this Jesus calls us to an ever more intimate relationship with him. How do we respond to Jesus' gift of himself?

Pope Francis addressed this question in his morning homily on September 26, 2013. He said that there are three languages in which to get to know Jesus. First, like Herod the Tetrarch of Galilee (King Herod's son), is curiosity. Herod asks about Jesus because Jesus seems to be causing trouble in the same manner as John the Baptist (Luke 9:7–9). Pope Francis remarks that if you want to get to know Jesus, it will not be a peaceful journey. Knowing Jesus will seem to create more problems in your life. And that is actually the first step in getting to know Jesus well.

A second way we can get to know Jesus, according to Pope Francis, is to study the *Catechism of the Catholic Church*. Through this study we can understand who Jesus is as the Son of God who came to save us. We can learn about the history of salvation and the love of the Father. Pope Francis then asks how many people have read the Catechism, although it was published twenty years ago. But the knowledge of Jesus we learn in the Catechism is "head" knowledge, and in itself it is not enough. And this leads to the third way of knowing Jesus:

> Yes, you have to come to know Jesus in the Catechism—but it is not enough to know Him with the mind: it is a step. However, it is necessary to get to know Jesus in dialogue with Him, talking with Him in prayer, kneeling. If you do not pray, if you do not talk with Jesus, you do not know Him. You know things about Jesus, but you do not go with that knowledge, which He gives your heart in prayer. Know Jesus with the mind—the study of the Catechism: know Je-

sus with the heart—in prayer, in dialogue with Him. This helps us a good bit, but it is not enough. There is a third way to know Jesus: it is by following Him. Go with Him, walk with Him." [114]

Ultimately, to really know Jesus, we must walk with him, to know him through our actions on behalf of others.

One cannot know Jesus without getting oneself involved with Him, without betting your life [on] Him. When so many people—including us—pose this question: "But, who is He?" The Word of God responds, "You want to know who He is? Read what the Church tells you about Him, talk to Him in prayer and walk the street with him. Thus, will you know who this man is." This is the way! Everyone must make his choice. [115]

This leads us to Pope Francis' homily on the Feast of Saint Ignatius Loyola. If we want to commit ourselves to walking with Jesus, we can reflect on the fundamental questions for all Christians in *The Spiritual Exercises*: What have I done for Christ? What am I doing for Christ? What must I do for Christ?

Christ Our Lord, the eternal King, calls each one of us, saying: "to anyone, then, who chooses to join me, I offer nothing but a share in my hardships; but if he follows me in suffering he will assuredly follow me in glory" (*EE,* 95); to be won over by Christ to offer to this King our whole person and our every endeavor (cf. *EE,* 96); saying to the Lord that we intend to do our utmost for the more perfect service and greater praise of his Majesty, putting up with all injustice, all abuse, all poverty (cf *EE,* 98). But at this moment my thoughts turn to our brother in Syria. Letting Christ make us his own always means straining forward to what lies ahead, to the goal of Christ (cf. Phil 3:14), and it also means asking oneself with truth and sincerity: what have I done for Christ? What am I doing for Christ? What must I do for Christ? (cf. *EE*, 53). [116]

On his pilgrimage to Assisi, Pope Francis retold the story of how Francis of Assisi came to answer those questions. As we have seen, the young Francis Bernardone spent his time and his father's money carelessly as the life of the party and following his dreams of knighthood, which led to personal disaster. Pope Francis traced the narrative that led to Francis of Assisi's radical change to lead a life imitating the poverty of Christ and one dedicated to the poor:

> Where did Francis's journey to Christ begin? It began with the gaze of the crucified Jesus. With letting Jesus look at us at the very moment that he gives his life for us and draws us to himself. Francis experienced this in a special way in the Church of San Damiano, as he prayed before the cross which I too will have an opportunity to venerate. On that cross, Jesus is depicted not as dead, but alive! Blood is flowing from his wounded hands, feet and side, but that blood speaks of life. Jesus' eyes are not closed but open, wide open: he looks at us in a way that touches our hearts. The cross does not speak to us about defeat and failure; paradoxically, it speaks to us about a death which is life, a death which gives life, for it speaks to us of love, the love of God incarnate, a love which does not die, but triumphs over evil and death. When we let the crucified Jesus gaze upon us, we are re-created, we become "a new

creation." Everything else starts with this: the experience of transforming grace, the experience of being loved for no merits of our own, in spite of our being sinners. That is why Saint Francis could say with Saint Paul: "Far be it for me to glory except in the cross of our Lord Jesus Christ" (Gal 6:14). [117]

In light of this, where do we find Jesus in everyday life? As we have seen, Pope Francis traces the journey through curiosity, contemplation, and the close study of the *Catechism*. But these are the first steps. To grow in a close relationship with Jesus is to encounter him in the wounds of the world. Pope Francis makes this clear in his homily on the Feast of Saint Thomas the Apostle, which tells the story of Thomas' encounter with the resurrected Jesus. Pope Francis observes that Thomas recognized Jesus as Lord when he gazed on Jesus' open wounds (John 20:24–29).

We gaze on the wounds of Jesus today when we gaze on the wounds of our brothers and sisters.

We find Jesus' wounds in carrying out works of mercy, giving to our body—the body—the soul too, but—I stress—the body of your wounded brother, because he is hungry, because he is thirsty, because he is naked because it is humiliated, because he is a slave, because he's in jail because he is in the hospital. Those are the wounds of Jesus today. And Jesus asks us to take a leap of faith, towards Him, but through these His wounds. "Oh, great! Let's set up a foundation to help everyone and do so many good things to help." That's important, but if we remain on this level, we will only be philanthropic. We need to touch the wounds of Jesus, we must caress the wounds of Jesus, we need to bind the wounds of Jesus with tenderness, and we have to kiss the wounds of Jesus, and this literally. Just think of what happened to Saint Francis, when he embraced the leper? The same thing that happened to Thomas: his life changed." [118]

MERCY, FORGIVENESS, AND PEACE

When Pope Francis made his visit to Saint Mary Major, in Rome, to venerate the image of Mary, he also took the opportunity to speak to the priests who listen to confessions throughout the day. He counseled them to always be merciful, that those confessing their sins need mercy.

Pope Francis' homilies leading up to and celebrating Holy Week gave him the opportunity to emphasize God's mercy and forgiveness. He made it clear that there should be no hesitation on the part of people celebrating the sacrament of reconciliation, because they are being met by a forgiving and merciful God: "This is also the great benefit of confession as a sacrament: evaluating case by case and discerning what is the best thing for a person to do who seeks God and grace. The confessional is not a torture chamber, but the place in which the Lord's mercy motivates us to do better." [119]

Pope Francis celebrated his first Sunday Mass after his election at Saint Anna parish in the Vatican. His homily for the day was on John 8:1–11, the woman caught in adultery. The great example that he takes from Jesus' words and actions is the value of mercy: "And Jesus has this message for us: mercy. I think—and I say it with humility—that this is the Lord's most powerful message: mercy. It was he himself who said: 'I did not come for the righteous.' The righteous justify themselves.

Go on, then, even if you can do it, I cannot! But they believe they can. 'I came for sinners'" (*Mk* 2:17). [120]

God especially calls on those who believe that they are beyond his mercy.

> It is not easy to entrust oneself to God's mercy, because it is an abyss beyond our comprehension. But we must! "Oh, Father, if you knew my life, you would not say that to me!" "Why, what have you done?" "Oh, I am a great sinner!" "All the better! Go to Jesus: he likes you to tell him these things!" He forgets, he has a very special capacity for forgetting. He forgets, he kisses you, he embraces you and he simply says to you: "Neither do I condemn you; go, and sin no more" (*Jn* 8:11). That is the only advice he gives you. After a month, if we are in the same situation . . . Let us go back to the Lord. The Lord never tires of forgiving: never! It is we who tire of asking his forgiveness. Let us ask for the grace not to tire of asking forgiveness, because he never tires of forgiving. [121]

RECONCILIATION AND PEACE

Having arrived at personal peace with the Lord, believers are more capable of being peacemakers with one another, their communities, and the world. Pope Francis has made clear how peace in the world, especially in Syria and the Middle East, is a priority concern for his papacy. He speaks for peace on every opportunity: when he speaks to heads of state, in the general audiences, in his daily homilies, and, most dramatically, at the Vigil of Fasting and Prayer, celebrated September 7, 2013, in Saint Peter's Square. He asked all Catholics to pray with him during this time. The event was streamed live from the Vatican around the world.

In his homily, Pope Francis presented an image of the world that all may hope for, a world in which men and women could live in healthy, intimate relationships and there would be peace between peoples and nations. The world we live in is still a fabulous place, given to us by God, but what use have we made of these gifts? All too often we have squandered and accumulated them in orgies of self-indulgence. The human family lives in fear that expresses itself clutching the power of money and affluence, indifferent to the poverty of their less fortunate brothers and sisters.

> Even today, we let ourselves be guided by idols, by selfishness, by our own interests, and this attitude persists. We have perfected our weapons, our conscience has fallen asleep, and we have sharpened our ideas to justify ourselves. As if it were normal, we continue to sow destruction, pain, death! Violence and war lead only to death, they speak of death! Violence and war are the language of death! [122]

We have seen in the life of Francis of Assisi his total commitment to promoting peace within the Christian community and with the Muslim world. This work of peace for him was for Christians first to be reconciled to themselves in the manner that Pope Francis has discussed. On his pilgrimage to Assisi, the pope highlighted Saint Francis' teaching on peace.

Pope Francis reminds Christians that those who follow Christ receive true peace that only Christ can give. The peace that Saint Francis teaches us is born of the love of the cross. It is the peace that the resurrected Jesus shares with us in John 29:19–20, when he shows his wounded hands and side.

> Franciscan peace is not something saccharine. Hardly! That is not the real Saint Francis! Nor is it a kind of pantheistic harmony with forces of the cosmos . . . That is not Franciscan either; it is a notion some people have invented! The peace of Saint Francis is the peace of Christ, and it is found by those who "take up" their "yoke," namely, Christ's commandment: Love one another as I have loved you (cf. Jn 13:34; 15:12). This yoke cannot be borne with arrogance, presumption or pride, but only with meekness and humbleness of heart. [123]

Pope Francis asks Saint Francis to intercede for us that we may be instruments of the peace that has been brought to us by Jesus.

MISSION TO THE PERIPHERIES

In our review of the lives of Saint Francis of Assisi and Saint Ignatius Loyola we saw that after their profound conversions to Jesus Christ, their greatest desire was to take his Word to the borders of their societies. Both desired to go to the Holy Land, which was under Muslim control. Both wanted to preach to the Muslims and to bring them to Christ. Saint Francis succeeded in his desire to preach when he traveled to Egypt to meet with Sultan al-Kamil. Ignatius made a pilgrimage to the Holy Land and wanted to return with his new Jesuit brothers. However, the early Jesuits were prevented by war and political circumstances from fulfilling their desire. They instead went to Rome to offer their services to the pope.

Both Saint Francis and Saint Ignatius served at the borders of their own societies, with their first impulse to serve the poor, the sick, those who lived on the edges of life, alienated from all who were better off. Both wanted to bring the Gospel to those who were not served. For Saint Francis and his followers, it was towns and villages ill served by an aristocratic Church, while Saint Ignatius taught children, served in hospitals, and cared for the poor. Eventually, as superior of the new community, he promoted the establishment of colleges and universities to address the needs of an increasingly literate laity.

Pope Francis wanted to be a missionary to Japan, but he was not given permission by his Jesuit superiors to do so, primarily because of his health issues. But in his episcopal ministry he served what was for him a new mission field: the poor communities of Argentina, whom he visited regularly. As bishop and archbishop he had focused his energies on sending priests to serve them. As Archbishop Bergoglio, he had also entered into dialogue with other Christian and Jewish communities, seeking common ground in working for the good of society. In his presentation to the Cardinals before the conclave, he stated clearly that moving toward the borders of society with the Word of God and the care of Jesus Christ must be the first priority of the Church.

In his general audience on March 27, 2013, Pope Francis emphasized that meditation on the cross was not simply a private affair with the Christian thanking Jesus for what he has done for us.

> Living Holy Week means entering ever more deeply into the logic of God, into the logic of the Cross, which is not primarily that of suffering and death, but rather that of love and of the gift of self which brings life. It means entering into the logic of the Gospel. Following and accompanying Christ, staying with him, demands "coming out of ourselves," requires us to be outgoing;

> to come out of ourselves, out of a dreary way of living faith that has become a habit, out of the temptation to withdraw into our own plans which end by shutting out God's creative action. [124]

We are called to come out of ourselves, because this is what God has done for us.

> God came out of himself to come among us, he pitched his tent among us to bring to us his mercy that saves and gives hope. Nor must we be satisfied with staying in the pen of the 99 sheep if we want to follow him and to remain with him; we too must "go out" with him to seek the lost sheep, the one that has strayed the furthest. Be sure to remember: coming out of ourselves, just as Jesus, just as God came out of himself in Jesus and Jesus came out of himself for all of us. [125]

CONCLUSION

Pope Francis does not want us to admire him from a distance. In his words and actions he is giving all Christians an example of what it means to be a follower of Jesus Christ today. He does not want the people to shout his name, but to shout the name of Jesus. We can marvel at his words and deeds, but more important, we can recognize that the God whom Pope Francis meets in prayer every day is the God who meets us when we rise, and who calls us each day to be who he is calling us to be.

QUESTIONS

According to Pope Francis, what is the source of Christian joy?

How can we come closest to finding Jesus today?

Why does Pope Francis tell us never to tire of asking for forgiveness?

How does Pope Francis' attitude toward Muslims reflect that of Saint Francis?

Why is it so important to come out of ourselves and move to the periphery?

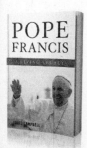

CHAPTER 12

WITNESSING GOD'S GRACE IN TIME

The Holy Spirit raises up the saints and disciples in every generation, calling them to address the needs of their time. Saint Francis of Assisi, Saint Ignatius Loyola, and Pope Francis are three men of the Church witnessing to God's grace.

SAINT FRANCIS OF ASSISI grew up a privileged member of his society. He was born into a wealthy merchant family that was stretching the class boundaries of their society. It was the beginning of the market economy, when wealth was measured not only in land, but in the hard cash earned by these first generations of capitalists. While the rich thrived and worked to increase their fortunes, the poor and the sick were increasingly left behind. Those suffering on the borders of society were left out. Growing up, Saint Francis took advantage of all the opportunities his family provided. He was the life of every party for his peers, and went to war seeking glory, wearing glittering armor and riding an expensive horse. Instead of victory and worldly honor, he suffered defeat and humiliation as a prisoner of war. His worldly hopes shattered, Francis discovered a new life in Jesus before the cross in San Damiano and among the lepers and outcasts of his world.

We have traced Francis' journey, from discovering God's mercy in the lepers he served to his vision of building God's Church as he meditated on the open wounds of Jesus Christ at San Damiano. After he renounced his family, he attracted others, and soon he had a community, which he sent out to proclaim the Gospel in the towns and village squares.

Francis and his followers taught what it meant to be Christian in the highly structured medieval society. In a day of complex and learned sermons, they brought the simple truths of the Gospel to the marketplace. In a time when lepers and others in need were ignored, they brought personal care to individuals and groups, letting them know how each was precious in the sight of God; when rigid social classes ruled the city and countryside, Francis established a community of equals, in which each was judged by his gifts and not by his titles; when fratricidal war and crusades against Islam were the societal norm, Francis and his followers not only taught the peace of the Lord, but did all they could to bring peace and reconciliation to troubled situations in towns and villages. Francis placed his own life on the line to reach out to the Islamic rulers in Egypt, earning their respect. The Franciscan legacy continues his work today.

SAINT IGNATIUS LOYOLA was born into a noble Basque family and was trained as a courtier and soldier in the court of Spain. He lived in a world of expanding horizons, when Spain was growing into a worldwide empire. One of his older brothers died while accompanying Balboa on his voyage of discovery to the Pacific Ocean. Due to the invention of a movable-type printing press, the intellectual world was also expanding, with the publication and distribution of printed books—romance, history, theological, devotional, and lives of the saints. These books fed the intellectual curiosity of the more literate and critical population, who now had access to many sources of knowledge, beyond the simple handing down of learning through oral tradition. The Church at this time was in need of reform due to financial and other abuses, which led to the Protestant revolt begun by Martin Luther in 1517.

Ignatius was an ambitious and well-respected courtier with dreams of military glory. These dreams ended when a cannonball shattered one leg and severely wounded the other during a siege in Pamplona, Spain. During his long convalescence, Ignatius read the only available books: a life of Jesus and lives of the saints. In his reflections and daydreams as he continued to read the books, Ignatius began to experience a conversion in his attitudes toward life. His old dreams of military and romantic success began to dry up, and he grew in a new enthusiasm for following the path of Saint Francis of Assisi and Saint Dominic as a disciple of Jesus.

Ignatius' new journey led him to a time of penance and reconciliation in Monserrat, further spiritual development and visions in Manresa, the beginnings of *The Spiritual Exercises*, a pilgrimage to the Holy Land, and finally back to school to learn theology, which led to ordination. Like Francis of Assisi, Ignatius attracted a group of talented young men, who would form the core of the Society of Jesus. In the difficult time of the Reformation, they placed themselves in service to the pope, and worked to meet the educational and social needs of the Church.

Ignatius' leadership gifts and training gave him the ability to address the issues of his time. With the printed book came the development of a more introspective spirituality based on meditation on texts and the examination of where a person as an individual fit into the more comprehensive plan of God for the Church and for the world. Through *The Spiritual Exercises* Ignatius developed a reliable method for care of the soul on a one-on-one basis. In the developing world of polemics based on study and research, Ignatius and his followers all were educated, receiving their master's degrees in theology as they prepared for the priesthood. They were up on the latest techniques, and one of Ignatius' first actions on becoming father general was to purchase a printing press. He was an outstanding administrator, and the number of Jesuits had grown from eight to a thousand by the time of his death. While early Jesuits were consultants for the Council of Trent, Ignatius also kept them on the borders, telling his priests to make sure they spent the mornings instructing children.

In response to the request from the King of Portugal, Ignatius sent his closest friend, Francis Xavier, to India and beyond as a missionary to the expanding world. Ignatius would be the first of many, including distinguished missionaries like Matteo Ricci and Roberto de Nobili, who entered into dialogue with the religious and social leaders of the better educated of the Asian world. Among the missionaries in the Americas would be Saints Isaac Jogues and René Goupil and their companions in North America, and Saint Peter Claver in Colombia.

Neither did Ignatius forget the poor, working in hospitals and establishing homes for women in need. Because of their educational gifts, the Jesuits were also pioneers in lay education. Many schools for laity were established while Ignatius still lived, with many more throughout the Indies and Americas in the decades that followed.

POPE FRANCIS

Early in the presidency of Ronald Reagan, there was a front lawn meeting at the White House with elementary school teachers. The text of the reporters' commentary was critical of some of the president's policies. However, the president's staff was delighted with the story. When asked why, they said, Look what is on the screen. No matter what the commentary said, the images on the screen were uniformly positive: the president celebrating with teachers. This is what the viewers would remember.

In line with what both Francis of Assisi and Ignatius Loyola taught their followers, Pope Francis has begun by teaching through his actions and not simply his words. This is especially important in the visual world of instant communication and paparazzi. As many celebrities have discovered, there is little that they can do in public (and many times in what they think is the privacy of their homes) that is not immediately connected to a visual link for worldwide distribution. Pope Francis realized that his actions would have immediate impact on a worldwide audience. He showed that the papal ministry is not simply the presiding over liturgical celebrations and formal meetings. Papal communication has to be more than releasing institutional documents. For Pope Francis papal ministry is person-to-person, in which, as Bishop of Rome, he can enter into the lives of his people.

Pope Francis has to address many issues in the Church and the world. The Church is facing persecution in many countries, an increasingly aggressive secular environment in the West, and more belligerent criticism from atheists. The benefits of globalization of the economy are highly praised, with little thought for the people left behind. The deaths in the Mediterranean among those who are seeking better lives are an ongoing concern. Human trafficking is destroying the lives of so many young people, as is the saturation of illegal drugs in society. Pope Francis was well versed in all of these issues, having learned about them and discussed them in *The Aparecida Document.*

In the first days of his papal ministry, his actions in stopping the popemobile to bless a severely disabled man and to embrace a young girl made headlines in the world press. He celebrated Holy Thursday in a youth prison in Rome, washing the feet of twelve inmates, including two young women, one of whom was Muslim. His first visit outside Italy was to the island of Lampedusa to raise awareness of the plight of refugees seeking better lives. When he arrived in the town of Assisi, he first visited the Serafico Institute and spoke to and embraced a hundred people with disabilities, taking time to pay personal attention to each. These images present to the world a man who is following the example of Jesus. In his care and concern for the most unfortunate, people are also seeing a care and concern for those most loved by Jesus.

All of these actions give a new context to Pope Francis' words. He has taken advantage of a variety of communication outlets to reach the people. In his daily homilies at Mass in the Santa Marta guesthouse, he is providing an ongoing retreat for the world on the daily readings in the liturgy. He makes full use of Twitter to present daily reminders of God's love for all. When Pope Francis gives a prepared homily that has an official translation, he usually makes spontaneous comments, complementing the official words with personal examples. But the most radical departure from previous protocol is giving interviews to members of the press, who have the opportunity to ask questions that have not been previously cleared or censored.

While there have been some negative reactions to the spontaneity and what some perceive as careless comments in these interviews, they fit into Pope Francis' desire for the Church to not simply carry out self-serving internal conversations but to reach out to the world in dialogue. There will be mistakes, but he would rather see mistakes made and corrected than communication cut off.

THREE AGES, THREE DISCIPLES

In the Christian world of the communion of saints, we know that the past is not truly gone, but lives in the shared grace of the saints in history who love us, inspire us, and are our companions on the journey. We have sketched Pope Francis' journey in the light of two of the saints who deeply inspire him and give him the courage to move forward.

In the papacies of recent generations we have had the examples of dedicated and holy men: Pius XII, Pope Saint John XXIII, Paul VI, John Paul I (albeit for only thirty-three days), Pope Saint John Paul II, Benedict XVI, and now Pope Francis. Each has brought to the tasks given to them by God unique gifts and perspectives, which they have given wholeheartedly to the ministry of the Church.

They are, of course, not the whole story. Christian life is carried out in the world by millions of faithful, in whom the love of God comes alive in their service to the world as symbols of God's grace. In this they all have been led by servant of the servants of God who, for all their limitations, have helped focus the Church in addressing the needs of the world.

Saint Francis, Saint Ignatius, and Pope Francis are models of God's call to each of us to listen, lead, reflect, and celebrate his grace in our lives, not delivered to us by snail mail, but coming as God himself into the core of our being.

QUESTIONS

How was Saint Francis a witness to God's presence in the medieval society of his time?

What gifts did Saint Ignatius Loyola bring to the needs of the Catholic world in the period of the Reformation?

How does Pope Francis teach with more than words?

What gifts do we bring to be a sign and symbol of God's grace in the world?

ABOUT THE AUTHOR

Jim Campbell has been a writer, speaker, and Christian adult educator for over forty years. Among his works are, *Old Testament Stories: A Catholic's Guide, and Mary* and the *Saints: Companions on the Journey.*

If you are interested in contacting the author
or inviting him to speak, please send an email to:
<u>everyman41@gmail.com</u>

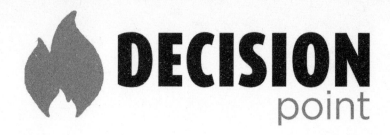
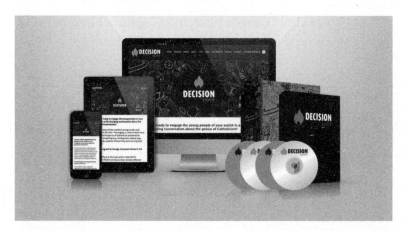

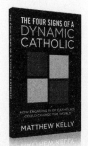

ENDNOTES

1. Englebert, Omer, *St. Francis of Assisi: A Biography* (Cincinnati: Franciscan Media, 2013), Kindle edition, 192–195.

2. Vauchez, Andre, Francis of Assisi: *The Life and Afterlife of a Medieval Saint* (New Haven, CT: Yale University Press, 2012), Kindle edition.

3. Ibid.

4. Ibid.

5. Spoto, Donald, *Reluctant Saint: The Life of Francis of Assisi* (New York: Penguin Compass, 2003), 3.

6. Thompson, Augustine, *Francis of Assisi: A New Biography* (Ithaca, NY: Cornell University Press, 2012), Kindle edition.

7. Many years ago I knew a young man who spent what was at that time the exorbitant amount of one hundred dollars on a pair of shoes. When the young man arrived at home, his parents criticized him for spending so much. However, when a well-to-do neighbor dropped in for a visit, the father brought out the receipt for the shoes, complaining about his son's extravagance. What was also obvious was that he was proud to be able to afford the expense.

8. Spoto, *Reluctant Saint,* 22–3.

9. In his study of Francis of Assisi, G. K. Chesterton notes: "While he was selling velvet and fine embroideries to some solid merchant of the town, a beggar came imploring alms; evidently in a somewhat tactless manner. It was a rude and simple society and there were no laws to punish a starving man for expressing his need for food, such as have been established in a more humanitarian age; and the lack of any organized police permitted such persons to pester the wealthy without any great danger. Chesterton, G. K., *St. Francis of Assisi* (Mineola, NY: Dover Publications, 2012), Kindle edition.

10. Spoto, *Reluctant Saint,* 36.

11. Vauchez, *Francis of Assisi.*

12. Spoto, *Reluctant Saint*, 60.

13. Vauchez, *Francis of Assisi.*

14. Thompson, *Francis of Assisi.*

15. The story is told in Paul Moses, *The Saint and the Sultan: The Crusades, Islam, and Francis of Assisi's Mission of Peace* (New York: Doubleday Religion, 2009).

16. *Wikipedia*, s. v. "Custodian of the Holy Land," last modified December 1, 2013, http://en.wikipedia.org/wiki/Custodian_of_the_Holy_Land.

17. Thompson, *Francis of Assisi*.

18. Vauchez, *Francis of Assisi*.

19. Englebert, *St. Francis of Assisi,* 4279–302.

20. Francis of Assisi and Clare of Assisi, *Francis and Clare: The Complete Works,* trans. Regis J. Armstrong and Ignatius C. Brady (New York: Paulist Press, 1982).

21. Vauchez, *Francis of Assisi*.

22. Delio, Ilia, *Franciscan Prayer* (Cincinnati: St. Anthony Messenger Press, 2004), Kindle edition, 822–32. 23. Vauchez, *Francis of Assisi*.

24. Ibid.

25. Ibid.

26. Ibid.

27. Delio, *Franciscan Prayer*.

28. Vauchez, *Francis of Assisi*.

29. Englebert, *St. Francis of Assisi,* 925–9.

30. Vauchez, *Francis of Assisi*.

31. Delio, *Franciscan Prayer*.

32. Horan, Daniel, *Francis of Assisi and the Future of Faith* (Phoenix: Tau Publishing, 2012), Kindle edition, 1489–94.

33. Englebert, *St. Francis of Assisi,* 1521–4.

34. Ibid., 1514–7.

35. Pope Francis, "Morning Homily," November 7, 2012.

36. Vauchez, *Francis of Assisi*.

37. Ibid.

38. Ibid.

39. Ibid.

40. Thompson, *Francis of Assisi*.

41. Ibid.

42. Horan, *Francis of Assisi and the Future of Faith.*

43. An indulgence is the taking away of the temporal punishment due to sins that have already been forgiven. A person may practice a devotion or good works that lessens this temporal punishment for themselves or others. A this time a contribution of money to the Church may also secure an indulgence for oneself or those who have died, lessening the temporal punishment. The scandal at the time of Luther was the blatant sale of indulgences in a carnival atmosphere without devotional sincerity.

44. Bokenkotter, Thomas, *A Concise History of the Catholic Church* (New York: Doubleday Religious Publishing Group, 2007), Kindle edition, 3249.

45. Ibid.

46. Ibid.

47. Ibid.

48. Modras, Ronald. *Ignatian Humanism: A Dynamic Spirituality for the Twenty-First Century* (Chicago: Loyola Press, 2004), Kindle edition, 902–6.

49. Ibid., 957–61.

50. Philip Caraman, *Ignatius Loyola: A Biography of the Founder of the Jesuits* (New York: Harper and Row, 1990) 6–7.

51. Hugo Rahner, *The Spirituality of St. Ignatius Loyola: An Account of Its Historical Development* (Westminster, MD: Newman Press, 1953), 6.

52. Caraman, *Ignatius Loyola,* 15.

53. Ibid., 21.

54. Ibid., 23.

55. Ignatius of Loyola, *Personal Writings,* ed. Joseph Munitiz (New York: Penguin Classics, 1997), Kindle edition.

56. Ibid.

57. Caraman, *Ignatius Loyola,* 27.

58. Ignatius of Loyola, *Personal Writings.*

59. Ibid.

60. Caraman, *Ignatius Loyola,* 30.

61. Ignatius of Loyola, *Personal Writings.*

62. Ignatius also relates how when he left Montserrat, a member of the community hurried to catch up with him. The man asked Ignatius if he had given his clothes to a poor man. When he said yes, the man, in tears, thanked him, because the community had not believed the poor man's story, thinking he had stolen the clothes.

63. Rahner, *The Spirituality of St. Ignatius Loyola,* 8.

64. Ibid., 22.

65. Ignatius of Loyola, *Personal Writings.* We can note that Martin Luther in his monastic life was also the victim of scruples, unable to find any comfort in the hours he spent in the confessional. He would finally find release reading Romans 3:24–25, which states that Christ died for our sins and was raised for our justification.

66. Ibid.

67. Gilles Cusson, *Biblical Theology and the Spiritual Exercises* (St. Louis: Institute of Jesuit Resources, 1994), 59.

68. Rahner, *The Spirituality of St. Ignatius Loyola,* 52.

69. Caraman, *Ignatius Loyola,* 50.

70. Ignatius of Loyola, *Personal Writings.*

71. Ibid.

72. Modras, *Ignatian Humanism.*

73. Caraman, *Ignatius Loyola,* 87.

74. Modras, *Ignatian Humanism.*

75. V General Conference of the Bishops of Latin America and the Caribbean, *Concluding Document* (2007), 12.

76. Ibid., 14

77. Ibid., 36

78. Ibid., 46

79. Ibid., 61

80. Chanda, Nayan, and Susan Froetschel, eds., *A World Connected: Globalization in the 21st Century* (New Haven, CT: Yale Center for the Study of Globalization, 2012), Kindle edition, 2286–9.

81. V General Conference of the Bishops of Latin America and the Caribbean, Concluding Document, 78.

82. Ibid., 66.

83. Tornielli, Andrea, Francis: Pope of a New World (San Francisco: Ignatius Press, 2013), Kindle edition, 814–7.

84. Tornielli, Andrea, "Rosa Margherita, Francis' 'Theologian' Grandmother," Vatican Insider, March 25, 2013, http://vaticaninsider.lastampa.it/en/the-vatican/detail/articolo/bergoglio-papa-el-papa-pope-23550/.

85. Ibid.

86. Rubin, Sergio, and Francesca Ambrogetti, Pope Francis: Conversations with Jorge Bergoglio: His Life in His Own Words (New York: Penguin Group, 2013), Kindle edition.

87. Rubin and Ambrogetti, Pope Francis.

88. Tornielli, Francis: Pope of a New World, 863–4.

89. Rubin and Ambrogetti, Pope Francis.

90. Ibid.

91. Ibid.

92. Tornielli, Francis: Pope of a New World, 978–80.

93. For a complete discussion of these years see: Tornielli, Andrea, "A Priest Under the Dictatorship," in Francis: Pope of a New World, 972–1105. See also: Vallely, Paul, Pope Francis: Untying the Knots (London: Bloomsbury Publishing, 2013), Kindle edition.

94. Rubin and Ambrogetti, Pope Francis.

95. Ibid.

96. Ibid.

97. John L. Allen Jr., "Pope Francis Gets His 'Oxygen' from the Slums," National Catholic Reporter, April 7, 2013, http://ncronline.org/blogs/francis-chronicles/pope-francis-gets-his-oxygen-slums.

98. Ibid.

99. Staff of The Wall Street Journal, Pope Francis: From the End of the Earth to Rome (New York: HarperCollins, 2013), Kindle edition, 103–113.

100. Tornielli, Francis: Pope of a New World.

101. Author, "Article Title," Rome Reports, April 6, 2013, www.webaddress.com. {Pls add missing info}

102. Pope Francis, *Encountering Christ: Homilies, Letters, and Addresses of Cardinal Jorge Bergoglio* (New Rochelle, NY: Scepter Publishers, 2013), Kindle Edition, 682–7.

103. Ibid.

104. The assignments he received were as a member of the Congregation for Divine Worship and the Discipline of the Sacraments, the Congregation for the Clergy, the Congregation for Institutes of Consecrated Life and Societies of Apostolic Life, the Pontifical Council for the Family, and the Pontifical Commission for Latin America.

105. Rubin and Ambrogetti, *Pope Francis*.

106. Ibid.

107. Bunson, Matthew E., *Pope Francis* (Huntington, IN: Our Sunday Visitor, 2013), Kindle edition.

108. The Western Schism (1378–1417) was a tragic period in the Church when there were two popes who claimed authority over the Catholic Church. One pope was in Rome; the second, in the French city of Avignon, where the papacy had moved in 1309. Attempts to heal the schism generally failed, and the situation got worse when a third pope was elected in 1409. The issue was finally resolved at the Council of Constance (1414–1418). The contending popes in Avignon and Rome resigned and a new pope, Martin V, was elected.

109. "Bergoglio's Intervention: A Diagnosis of the Problems in the Church," Vatican Radio, March 27, 2013, http://en.radiovaticana.va/news/2013/03/27/bergoglios_intervention:_a_diagnosis_of_the_problems_in_the_church/en1-677269.

110. Gibson, David, and Alessandro Speciale, "Pope Francis Explains Why He Chose His Name, Urges a 'Church of the Poor,'" Religion News Service, March 16, 2013, http://www.religionnews.com/2013/03/16/pope-francis-explains-why-he-chose-his-name-urges-a-church-of-the-poor/.

111. Pope Francis, "Homily of the Holy Father Pope Francis: 'Missa Pro Ecclesia' with the Cardinal Electors," Libreria Editrice Vaticana, March 14, 2013.

112. Pope Francis, "Homily of Pope Francis: Celebration of Palm Sunday of the Passion of Our Lord," Libreria Editrice Vaticana, March 24, 2013.

113. Pope Francis, "General Audience," Libreria Editrice Vaticana, April 10, 2013.

114. Pope Francis, "Knowing Jesus: Morning Meditation in the Chapel of the *Domus Sanctae Marthae,*" Libreria Editrice Vaticana, September 26, 2013.

115. Ibid.

116. Pope Francis, "Homily of Holy Father Francis on the Occasion of the Feast of Saint Ignatius," Libreria Editrice Vaticana, July 31, 2013.

117. "Pope's Homily for Solemn Mass in Assisi," Vatican Radio, October 3, 2013.

118. Pope Francis, "Touching the Wounds of Jesus: Morning Meditation in the Chapel of the *Domus Sanctae Marthae,*" Libreria Editrice Vaticana, July 3, 2013.

119. Spadaro, Antonio, "A Big Heart Open to God," *America*, September 30, 2013.

120. Pope Francis, "Homily of Pope Francis: Holy Mass in the Parish of St. Anna in the Vatican," Libreria Editrice Vaticana, March 17, 2013.

121. Ibid.

122. Pope Francis, "Words of Holy Father Francis: Vigil of Prayer for Peace," Libreria Editrice Vaticana, September 7, 2013.

123. "Pope's Homily for Solemn Mass in Assisi."

124. Pope Francis, "General Audience," Libreria Editrice Vaticana, March 27, 2013.

125. Ibid.

THE
DYNAMIC CATHOLIC
INSTITUTE

[MISSION]

To re-energize the Catholic Church
in America by developing world-class
resources that inspire people to
rediscover the genius of Catholicism.

[VISION]

To be the innovative leader in the
New Evangelization helping Catholics
and their parishes become
the-best-version-of-themselves.

◼◼ DynamicCatholic.com
Be Bold. Be Catholic.®

The Dynamic Catholic Institute
5081 Olympic Blvd • Erlanger, KY 41018
phone: 859–980–7900
email: info@DynamicCatholic.com